Impact Therapy

Ed Jacobs, Ph.D.

D1557996

IMPACT Therapy

Ed Jacobs, Ph.D.

To Carolyn,

Enjoy!

E. Jacobs

PAR Psychological Assessment Resources, Inc.
P.O. Box 998/Odessa, Florida 33556

Library of Congress Cataloging-in-Publication Data
Jacobs, Edward E., 1944–
        Impact Therapy/ Ed Jacobs.
              p.   cm.
        ISBN 0-911907-18-1
        1. Psychotherapy.   I. Title.
    RC480.5.J23   1994
    616.89' 14--dc20   94-32320
                                                                   CIP

Printed in the United States of America.   2 3 4 5 6 7 8 9   Reorder #RO-2847

Acknowledgments

Many people have influenced and encouraged me in my development as a counselor and counselor educator. Three professors at Florida State University, Harman Burck, Bob Reardon, and Jim Croake, were particularly helpful and encouraging when I was trying to figure out my approach to counseling. I thank them for allowing me the freedom to explore counseling as it fit with my personality and beliefs about the counseling process.

I also want to thank Pat Love for the long discussions that we had that led to the conceptualization of Impact Therapy and for her continued support of the work that I am doing. I want to thank Danie Beaulieu for her encouragement to develop the Impact Therapy model. Her enthusiasm for the approach and the name, Impact Therapy, helped me to decide that I should fully develop Impact Therapy and teach my approach to others via books and workshops.

I also want to thank Chris Schimmel for her work with the development of this book and Impact Therapy. I feel fortunate to have her as my associate. Special thanks goes to Jane Somers who served as much more than a copy editor for this book. Her constructive comments truly made the book much better. I greatly appreciate Jane's understanding of me and the project and her tremendous desire to make the book the best it can possibly be.

Thanks also to the people at PAR—Bob Smith, Serje Seminoff, and Sandy Schneider—for being great people to work with. They made the project enjoyable and better by being who they are.

Ed Jacobs
Impact Therapy Associates
Morgantown, West Virginia
August 1994

Table of Contents

Preface

This book is for counselors, social workers, and psychologists who work in schools, mental health agencies, treatment centers, rehabilitation centers, and crisis centers. *Impact Therapy* was written to help counselors work at a faster and more productive pace. *Impact Therapy* is for therapists working with all populations since it is very broad in its focus and deals with the counseling process and how clients learn. In this book, I discuss in detail my approach to counseling, which I call Impact Therapy. Impact Therapy can be useful with any client and is excellent with children, teenagers, and clients who are eager to work through whatever it is that is bothering them. Impact Therapy allows the therapist to bypass most resistance since the therapist is open to trying many different creative and engaging ways to reach the client. As you read the book, you will naturally want to think in terms of the specific population(s) with whom you work. Because I use examples from a wide range of settings, you should find numerous examples that relate to your specific population.

I have written this book for those who have been previously introduced to therapy through courses and training and who have knowledge of rapport building and counseling theory. Readers who do not have a strong background in basic skills should refer to one of the beginning texts on counseling by authors such as Cormier and Hackney (1993) or Egan (1994). Those who do not have a background in theory should refer to the primary sources on the various theories that are referenced throughout the book. I discuss some theories in brief and describe how Impact Therapy uniquely integrates concepts from them.

This is a rather short book because I describe an approach to counseling rather than a new theory of human behavior that needs to be explained in detail. I wrote the book because participants in my Impact Therapy workshops in recent years have asked me to put into writing the ideas and concepts regarding the counseling process that I have been teaching.

For the purpose of ease in reading, I have chosen to alternate the use of the pronouns "he" and "she" and "her" and "him" rather than the more awkward "she or he" and "him or her." I use both "therapy" and "counseling" and "counselor" and "therapist" interchangeably. I refer to the person in therapy as "client."

Impact Therapy has been very well received because it is practical, easy to grasp, and helpful in making counseling more productive. I am very excited about the possibilities of Impact Therapy and believe you will find this book to be informative, motivating, and helpful.

Chapter 1

Introduction

WHAT IS IMPACT THERAPY?

Impact Therapy is an approach to counseling that shows respect for the way clients learn, change, and develop. The emphasis is on making counseling clear, concrete, and thought provoking, rather than vague, abstract, and emotional. I developed Impact Therapy to be a multi-sensory approach which recognizes that change or impact comes from not only verbal, but also visual and kinesthetic exchanges. It is a type of brief therapy although it is different from the work of Watzlawick, Weakland, and Fisch who have developed a school of therapy called "Brief Therapy." Impact Therapy is a form of therapy that combines creative counseling techniques (Jacobs, 1992) and certain counseling theories. It provides the counselor with ways to frame the counseling process as well as ways to assess the progress of a session. This approach is action and insight oriented and often resolution oriented. I call my approach Impact Therapy because it emphasizes helping the client as much as possible in each session. The therapist is always trying to get to the core of the problem by not listening to unnecessary details and irrelevant stories. The impact therapist sees the goal of any therapy session as creating change or setting in motion the process for change.

Impact Therapy is a unique approach to counseling, integrating concepts from Rational Emotive Therapy (RET), Transactional Analysis (TA), Gestalt, and the counseling techniques that are discussed in *Creative Counseling Techniques: An Illustrated Guide* (Jacobs, 1992). The impact therapist uses RET and Gestalt therapy with creative props, drawings, and analogies in a very different manner than the way these theories are traditionally taught. The impact therapist uses the ego states from TA with chairs, drawings, movement, and in combination with RET in clear, concrete, and effective ways. Therapists who subscribe to Systems theory, Adlerian counseling, Reality Therapy, and most other theories should find Impact Therapy to be compatible. Impact Therapy serves as a solid bridge between theories and techniques and provides a clear way to understand the process and progress of a therapy session.

Impact Therapy is an empowering approach to therapy that shows great respect for the client. Impact Therapy calls for the client to be active, thinking, seeing, and experiencing during the session. Impact therapists try to help clients help themselves by getting the clients to think rationally about their issues. Challenging clients' self-talk and using analogies, props, movement, and additional chairs help make Impact Therapy sessions engaging and beneficial. Dependent relationships are rare in Impact Therapy since the counselor is always involving the client in many different ways. This involvement causes the client to have to think on his own rather than be dependent on the counselor. Thus, clients feel empowered but not dependent.

WHY IMPACT THERAPY?

Too often in my training workshops, I find that there is something missing from the "toolboxes" of counselors and therapists. Though counselors may be familiar with various theories and techniques, they do not succeed in being effective with clients; they do not have impact. Many counselors use a rather slow process of counseling where much time is spent building rapport and responding with reflections and clarifications. I see the benefit in this for some clients although I believe that, for the majority of clients, a faster and more active approach to counseling can be more beneficial. Too often clients are frustrated by the pace of their therapy. I hear far too many stories of clients who experienced counseling that was slow, not focused, and, most of all, not helpful. Impact Therapy, on the other hand, offers the practitioner ways to get more accomplished in a session.

Many counseling situations in mental health centers, drug and alcohol settings, and school settings demand that the counselor be able to engage the client rather quickly. Insurance and managed care companies are also demanding that therapy not be a long, drawn-out process. Impact Therapy responds to these demands and calls for the counselor to speed up the counseling process by following some basic steps. Impact Therapy gets clients thinking for themselves and thus promotes confidence and independence instead of the dependency which is sometimes found in other therapies. Certainly I acknowledge that there are many counseling issues that require a number of sessions, such as sexual abuse, grief, or recovery from an addiction to drugs or alcohol. Even with these kinds of cases, Impact Therapy can speed up the process since there is an emphasis on clients' moving through their issues rather than wallowing in them.

WHAT IS THE APPROACH USED IN IMPACT THERAPY?

The letters **RCFF** describe the therapeutic process of Impact Therapy and stand for **Rapport**, **Contract**, **Focus**, and **Funnel**. Most experts agree that counseling goes through stages, phases, or a process. Writers have labeled the stages in many different ways (Carkuff, 1987; Egan 1994; Ivey, 1994). Most of the writing is in regard to the stages of counseling over a series of sessions. Impact Therapy addresses the phases that any session should go through, whether it is the first session or the last session. The terms Rapport, Contract, Focus, and Funnel describe the phases of counseling as I see them. Viewing the counseling process in this way causes the therapist to always keep in mind that the purpose of the session is to focus and funnel so that there is impact. Impact Therapy emphasizes getting something accomplished.

RCFF is the heart of Impact Therapy. I make reference to the **RCFF** process throughout the book. **Understanding each of the four phases of RCFF is essential for conducting Impact Therapy.** Chapters 4, 5, 6, and 7 are devoted to these concepts, so I only briefly describe them here.

> **Rapport:** This is the relationship between the counselor and the client. Good rapport is essential for almost all counseling.

> **Contract:** This refers to the implicit or explicit agreement between the counselor and the client as to the goal or purpose of the entire session or portion of the session.

> **Focus:** Focusing the session means dealing with a specific topic or issue for a given length of time.

> **Funnel:** Funneling the session is discussing an issue in such a way that there is some new level of understanding or insight—that is, "taking it deeper."

Certainly at the end of every session, I spend a few minutes closing the session by having the client summarize what he learned and talk about how he will use the information gained in the session. I often use the closing to discuss possible tasks that the client can do between appointments that will be beneficial for him.

For group counseling, instead of **RCFF**, I refer to **PPFF**, which stands for **Purpose**, **Plan**, **Focus**, and **Funnel**. These phases are discussed in detail in chapter 9.

Purpose: Clarity of purpose is a must for good group leading. The leader has to be very clear as to why the group is meeting and the kind of group that is being led. Purpose determines everything else.

Plan: Good planning is essential for almost all groups and for all but the very experienced leader. Topics and activities should be considered ahead of time.

Focus: Focusing means directing the group to appropriate topics or issues. Knowing how to focus is a must for good group leadership.

Funnel: Funneling the group is discussing an issue in such a way that there is a new level of understanding or insight for the members. Funneling issues and topics is the most important phase of any group.

THE DEPTH CHART

The process, development, and progression of the counseling session is at the center of Impact Therapy since great emphasis is placed on focusing and funneling. One way to concretely view the counseling process and flow of a session is to use the Depth Chart (Jacobs, 1992). In Impact Therapy, the Depth Chart is a scale of *10-1* that serves as the basis for evaluating how in-depth the session is proceeding. A *10* indicates that the issue being dealt with is only being discussed on the surface. I consider any topic funneled to a level of *7* or below as having impact. The diagram on the following page provides a visual example of the Depth Chart. A session is charted where the topics of depression, work, and upbringing are discussed. The first two topics started at *10* and went to *8* and then back to a new topic. The therapist decided to focus and funnel the third topic, upbringing, so that the client would gain new insights about her childhood.

The Depth Chart can be used for any session and is a clear and concrete way to conceptualize the flow and impact of the session. By using this concept, impact therapists will develop a tendency to be more productive because they will want their sessions to funnel below *7*. Throughout the book, I refer to the Depth Chart when I talk about taking the session below *7*.

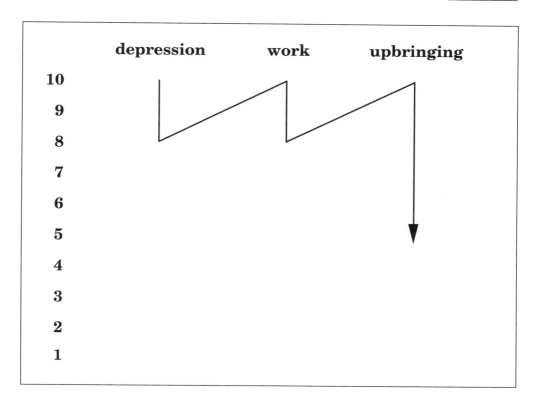

The diagram on the following page provides a visual representation of **RCFF** integrated with the Depth Chart. As illustrated, real impact occurs when the session is focused and then funneled below **7**.

CHARACTERISTICS OF AN EFFECTIVE IMPACT THERAPIST

Much has been written regarding the characteristics of an effective counselor (Gladding, 1988; Cormier & Cormier, 1991). It is important for any therapist to consider if she has the appropriate characteristics. Anyone concerned about whether he or she has the characteristics that are suitable for being an effective counselor should review some beginning texts that discuss this topic. In addition to what has been written, there are two more characteristics that I feel are necessary to be an effective impact therapist: creativity and courage.

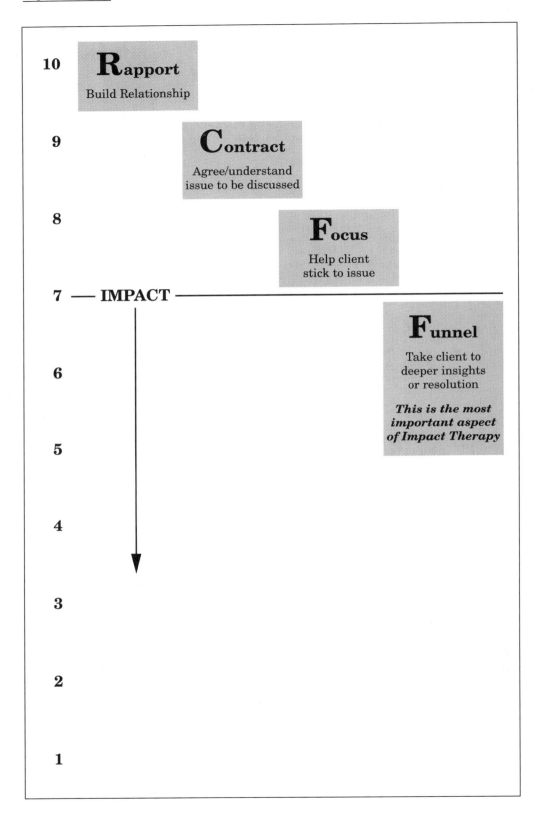

10 **R**apport

Build Relationship

9 **C**ontract

Agree/understand
issue to be discussed

8 **F**ocus

Help client
stick to issue

7 — IMPACT

Funnel

Take client to
deeper insights
or resolution

*This is the most
important aspect
of Impact Therapy*

6

5

4

3

2

1

Creativity

Impact therapists are creative in their approach to counseling. They are willing to try different strategies and techniques, such as the use of props, chairs, drawings, and movement, during the session in order to have impact. Impact therapists are willing to use such props as rubber bands, shields, filters, and small chairs to make the counseling more visual and concrete (see Jacobs, 1992). They also may have the client move around, sit on the floor, stand on chairs, or even stand in the corner. Impact therapists use stories, analogies, and fantasies in different ways during a session. Also, impact therapists are creative in trying different counseling formats, such as talking to the client daily, meeting in different settings, bringing in other therapists or someone with a similar problem (a current or former client who has or had a similar concern).

Courage

One needs courage to be an impact therapist because Impact Therapy requires a willingness to try many different techniques in order to have a meaningful session. The impact therapist has the courage to interrupt or stop clients when they are off on tangents or to stop destructive interactions in group, couple, and family counseling. Also, when necessary, the impact therapist is not afraid to confront a client or use language that gets the client's attention, such as "Look, if you come in and whine like a helpless kid, we won't accomplish anything. You're 37 years old, and sometimes you act more like you're 10. I want to help you, but you have to quit whining."

The impact therapist is willing to direct the session to difficult material, such as affairs, divorce, abuse, or anger. The therapist is comfortable talking about issues such as sex or death and is willing to ask very personal questions regarding these matters. Workshop participants have commented how afraid they were to ask personal questions—they felt they were prying. Good therapy is not prying; it is asking the questions that need to be asked in order to help the client.

The impact therapist tries to take clients into their issues and pain whereas many other therapists often back away or let their clients back off. The noncourageous counselor worries about hurting his clients' feelings and, therefore, plays it safe whereas the impact therapist knows that sometimes the therapy has to be temporarily painful in order to move the client through her unfinished business.

BELIEFS OF IMPACT THERAPY

Most theories of counseling are built on some basic principles. I subscribe to a number of the principles found in RET, TA, Gestalt, and Adlerian counseling, such as thoughts cause feelings; people communicate from different ego states; dealing with issues in the here-and-now is valuable; and all behavior is purposeful. Along with these beliefs are the core beliefs central to what I believe about counseling, clients, and therapists:

1. People don't change easily. Understanding this belief about human beings encourages the therapist to work hard during the session to make the session productive. The impact therapist will try many different therapeutic strategies, especially when she sees that what she is doing is not working. Believing that people don't change easily helps keep the counselor from getting angry at the client, getting discouraged, or giving up on the client. It is important to note that there will be times when the counselor has to accept the fact that certain clients are not willing or ready to change, so she should invest her energy in those who want to work on issues.

2. People don't mind being led when they are led well. This belief is extremely important, especially for those therapists leading groups. Often in training programs and in counseling texts, therapists are told not to take an active role when conducting an individual or group session. I disagree with this notion, and I encourage impact therapists to be active. A good, active therapist can create a positive climate for therapy. In groups, members will appreciate the leader who appropriately focuses the session, initiates activities, or helps members work on issues. (See chapter 8 for further discussion of this belief.)

3. The therapist is primarily responsible for the therapy. This belief is central to Impact Therapy. I realize that the client is ultimately responsible for the outcome of therapy and that any client can defeat even the best therapist, but I believe that the therapist is the person responsible for trying to make the session productive. Many therapists get lazy and turn the session over to their clients, with the result being that counseling never goes below **7**.

4. Counseling should be clear and concrete. For most clients, therapy is more productive when it is straightforward. The impact therapist works hard to make her counseling specific and focused by using theories in ways understandable to the client and by using props, chairs, drawings, analogies, and other creative techniques. Clients often tell me that they have seen other therapists and were never sure what was happening because the sessions were vague and disjointed.

5. Therapy should never be boring. Many therapists complain that counseling is boring. This in turn will lead to burnout on the part of any therapist. It is my belief that if the counselor is doing his job well, the session will be interesting because he will be using different strategies and creative techniques to take the session to **7** or below. Almost all counseling below **7** is interesting and engaging for both the client and the counselor. It is only when the therapist stops trying to have impact that the session has a chance to become boring. People tend to learn more and remember more when what they are doing is interesting to them. Thus, I believe that therapy should be interesting and not boring.

6. It is okay for the therapist to give advice when she understands the client's frame of reference and when the therapist's moral and religious values are not involved. I understand why training programs teach the idea of not giving advice, but unfortunately, this is sometimes taught incorrectly. Most often I hear counselors say that they were taught "never give advice" which simply is not a good guiding principle for counselors to believe. Experienced therapists quickly learn that giving advice sometimes is quite appropriate and helpful, especially in instances where the client does not seem to have any idea as to what to do regarding a given situation. Clients sometimes need help in managing their lives, and appropriate advice can be very beneficial and can prevent destructive behaviors. I encourage impact therapists to give advice cautiously but to give advice when the situation calls for it. When there is a moral or religious issue, such as affairs, divorce, or abortion, the therapist has to be very sure that he is not unethically imposing his own beliefs on the client.

7. Counselors' and clients' worth is never on the line. I include this as a core belief for two reasons. It is important that therapists do not think their worth goes up or down based on counseling outcomes. It is also good for the counselor to believe this about his clients since they so often attach worth to such things as appearance, intelligence, parenting skills, marital status, and job performance. The impact therapist has many different ways to show that the client's worth is never on the line.

8. An impact therapist must be mentally healthy. Conducting therapy in the manner that I am describing requires that the therapist is emotionally centered and well balanced. He should have worked through the majority of his issues and should handle remaining issues in a reasonable fashion. Impact therapists are able to read and understand people easily and are usually able to move a session rather quickly to a deeper level. Impact therapists are comfortable with many different kinds of clients, and clients usually feel comfortable with them. Impact Therapists enjoy the counseling profession, and their clients can sense their enjoyment, dedication, and desire to be helpful.

COMMON MISTAKES OF THERAPISTS

Throughout my 20 years of conducting workshops, I have discovered that there are a number of mistakes that counselors make, especially during their first few years of counseling. Many make these mistakes because of the way they were taught or because they emphasize listening and letting the client direct the session. These mistakes lead to counseling that is either not effective or only minimally effective. This book presents ideas on how to avoid these mistakes.

1. Reflecting much more than necessary. Counselors need to use reflection in their sessions. However, counselors in training are often given entire courses on how to reflect, which leads to the belief that reflection is the most important counseling technique in building rapport and encouraging change. Too often, clients hear a parroting back of what they said, causing them to more or less repeat themselves, thus wasting time. Many counselors listen to their clients and think, "What should I reflect back?" whereas the impact therapist thinks, "What response would be best to focus the client so as to have impact?" Reflection is useful when it helps build rapport, moves the session along, or gives the therapist time to think, but it is not helpful when it is used without considering if it is the best response in the given situation.

2. Listening to too many stories. All therapists are trained to listen to their clients, and often clients want to tell stories. The counseling mistake that is made is listening to more stories than is needed to make progress in the session. The impact therapist knows when to say to the client, "I think I have it. Let's begin to focus on helping you understand what is happening."

3. Rarely interrupting the client. Counselors are rarely taught to interrupt the client. Often clients are allowed to ramble for very long periods of time without the counselor intervening. There will be times when the counselor sees the need to focus on a certain point that the client is talking about but, believing that interrupting is always wrong, waits until the client finishes talking. By the time the client finishes, they have moved on to another topic.

Not only is it acceptable to interrupt the client when he is talking, many times it is best to interrupt. It is especially necessary to interrupt when the client is telling one story after another or is repeating the same content over again. Counselors who do not understand the necessity of interrupting the client waste valuable counseling time and often miss the opportunity for impact. When timed appropriately, I have found that clients do not feel offended but rather appreciate that I am trying to make the session meaningful.

4. Not focusing the session. Many therapists concentrate on listening and following their clients. They do not focus the session but rather wait for the client to provide the focus. This is a mistake. Many clients never focus, or they take a very long time to get focused; and, thus, the session is not productive. Impact therapists believe that it is their responsibility to focus the session and that lack of focus will equal lack of productivity.

5. Waiting too long to focus and funnel the session. Some counselors see counseling as a slow, relaxing, meandering process in which the client will delve into matters when he feels comfortable and ready. Some believe that the client should be in charge of when the session should focus and funnel. The impact therapist, however, tries to focus and funnel the session as soon as possible, given there is good rapport and a contract. She knows that impact most often occurs when there is enough time to fully discuss an issue.

6. Not using theory—using the "hope method" of counseling. The biggest mistake of many counselors is that they do not use theory because they did not learn one well enough to use it in a session. Too many counselors rely on being warm and empathetic, listening to their clients, and hoping they get better. The "hope method" is not good therapy. In chapter 2, I discuss why Impact Therapy is theory driven.

7. Making counseling boring. Therapists often make counseling boring by using boring techniques. They let the client ramble on about things that are not interesting to either the client or the counselor. They gather much more information than they need to by asking for all kinds of useless details and descriptions. Boring counselors rarely move, write, draw, or use any kind of visual prop. Active, creative counseling is much more productive and interesting for both the client and the counselor.

SUMMARY

Impact Therapy is an active approach to counseling that bridges theory and techniques. The process of Impact Therapy centers around **RCFF**: rapport, contract, focus, and funnel. The process of group Impact Therapy centers around **PPFF**: purpose, plan, focus, and funnel. The **Depth Chart** is very useful to Impact Therapists and is used to assess the focusing and funneling of a session. Two important characteristics of an impact therapist are creativity and courage. The core beliefs of Impact Therapy are (a) people don't change easily; (b) people don't mind being led when they are led well; (c) the therapist is primarily responsible for the therapy; (d) therapy should never be boring; (e) it is okay to give advice; (f) counselor's and client's worth is never on the line; and (g) impact therapists must be mentally healthy. Common mistakes of counselors include reflecting more than necessary, listening to too many stories, rarely interrupting the client, not focusing or waiting too long to focus the session, not using theory, or making counseling boring.

Chapter 2

The Five "Ts" of Impact Therapy

In chapter 1, I introduced you to Impact Therapy and why I think it is an important approach to counseling. In this chapter, I continue my description of Impact Therapy by discussing five key concepts that the impact therapist always has in mind: **theory**, **timing**, **teaching**, **training**, and **thinking**. Each of these concepts is an integral part of Impact Therapy. All sessions will include theory, timing, and thinking; and the majority of sessions will also include teaching and/or training.

THEORY

Impact Therapy is driven by theory. By theory driven, I mean that other therapists would be able to recognize the theory or theories being used if they were to observe the therapy. Unfortunately, many, if not most, therapists do not counsel from a theoretical framework. In workshops I conduct all over the country, the majority of counselors do not know theory well enough to take their clients below **5** on the Depth Chart. Counselors may be able to initiate counseling without theory; but to help clients with their guilt, shame, anger, hurt, and other deep-seated issues, counselors have to know theory and how to use it in counseling sessions. **Being a good therapist requires working hard to understand human behavior.** Theory helps counselors understand in a complex way what is going on with their clients and gives a road map as to what might be needed to help a person with his particular concern.

When doing intensive therapy, that is therapy at the **5** level or below, theory is absolutely needed. I lean toward Rational Emotive Therapy (RET), Transactional Analysis (TA), Adlerian, Gestalt, and Reality Therapy because these theories answer the questions about where feelings come from, why people engage in self-defeating and self-destructive behavior, why people fight, and why it is hard to change. Impact Therapy is an integration of these theories and other theories and is compatible with most therapy approaches, but not all. A therapist relying heavily on Person-Centered therapy or Psychoanalysis would not be comfortable using the techniques and ideas from Impact Therapy since those theories limit the response options of the therapist.

Because Impact Therapy is theory driven, I offer descriptions of the main theories of Impact Therapy and how they are used by the impact therapist. My overviews are brief since the reader should already have some knowledge of each of these theories.

RET and Impact Therapy

Of all the theories that I have learned during my 30 years of studying counseling, Rational Emotive Therapy (RET) has been the most helpful because it clarifies for me how we cause our feelings. I think every therapist should understand the basic premise of RET which is **thoughts cause feelings** which in turn cause behaviors. (An excellent source for further information on RET is *A Practitioner's Guide To Rational-Emotive Therapy* by Walen, DiGiuseppe, and Wessler [1992].)

Counseling is helping people change feelings and behaviors, and one of the best ways to do this is to help people change their thoughts and self-talk. RET uses an ABC model to describe where feelings come from, with A being the activating event, person, or situation; B is the beliefs, self-talk, or irrational ideas; and C is the consequence or feeling that results from B. Most people believe that A causes C, but **RET maintains that B causes C—that clients upset themselves by telling themselves things about events, situations, or people that are irrational, not true, or greatly exaggerated.** For instance, if a client came in having been called names by fellow students, an RET therapist would see the problem something like the example below.

Activating Event	A = Being called names
Beliefs	B = No one likes me. I'll never have any friends. I must be what they called me and that is awful. I can't stand it that they called me those names.
Consequences/Feelings	C = Bad

The RET therapist usually teaches the client the idea that it is his thoughts that cause how he feels. The therapist then disputes the client's self-talk by using various techniques to get the client to see that his self-talk is not true. Disputing the self-talk usually takes the form of challenging the accuracy of the client's beliefs. Using the example above, the RET therapist would say things such as "Is it true that no one likes you or that these people may not like you? Just because those kids do not want to be your friends, does that mean you will never have any friends? Do you believe that because they called you a name, it means that you are what they called you? If they called you a 'dumb ass,' would that make you a donkey? Which is true—that you can't stand it or that it does not feel good when people call you names?"

An RET therapist and an impact therapist both spend much time disputing the negative self-talk of clients by challenging the wording, logic, and false conclusions. The impact therapist very frequently adds visual and creative ways to dispute the client's self-talk. Because many clients remember more of what they see than what they hear, frequently the impact therapist writes out the sentences under two columns, **Not True** and **True** or **Irrational** and **Rational**. Written out, it would look something like the following example.

NOT TRUE	TRUE
No one likes me.	These kids do not like me, but others do.
I'll never have any friends.	I have some friends; I just may not be friends with these kids.
I must be what they called me.	People can't make me anything. Just because they call me some name, that doesn't make it true.
I can't stand it that they called me names.	I don't like to be called names, but I can stand it. I sure wish they didn't act they way they do.
Bad	Better

The impact therapist points out how the sentences on the left cause bad feelings where the sentences on the right lead to feeling better. Having the sentences written out is very helpful for the client and also helps to keep the session focused on changing the self-talk.

There are many other ways that the impact therapist integrates RET into Impact Therapy. Often, an impact therapist asks a client to rate something or someone, such as her job, spouse, brother, boss, or father, on a 1-10 scale. In the following example, the therapist has the client rate her boss. He then writes her rating of 4 on a flip chart and asks the client, "When you are around your boss, do you keep in mind that he's a 4, or do you get mad because he is not an 8 or a 10?"

<u>NOT TRUE</u>

He should be an 8!!
I can't stand it!

<u>TRUE</u>

Boss is a 4
I wish he were an 8.
I need to get my expectations in
  line with reality. He's a 4. I
  don't like it, but I can stand it.

The counselor tries to have impact by visually presenting the client's irrational ideas. Clients tend to remember ratings more when they are written.

Another creative use of RET has to do with having a client rate some aspect of his life over the last few years so that the client can see a trend of how things have declined. For example, seeing a visual graph of the decline in a marriage over the last few years can help the client see her irrational thought about the marriage getting better.

Example

Counselor: Let's look at a picture of your marriage. I want you to rate your marriage over the last few years on a 1-10 scale, with 10 being great and 1 being miserable. (*Client does this.*)

Counselor: When you tell me that you think things will get better, and the trend of your marriage looks like this, I tend to believe you are kidding yourself. Andy, you tell me how you see any hope as you look at this diagram.

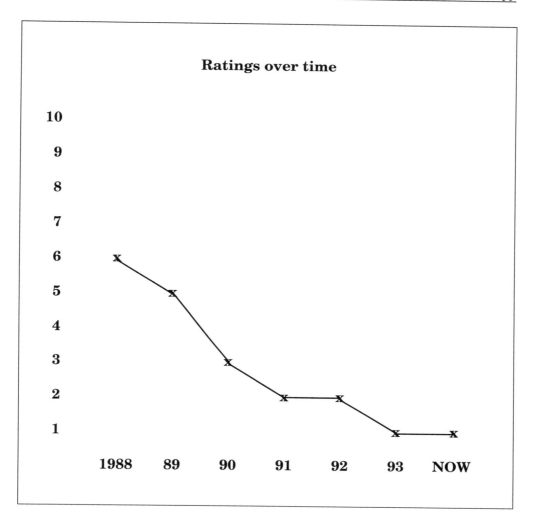

Ratings over time

Client: (*Stares at the drawing*) Seeing it like this makes it hard for me to hold on to any hope. I've never thought of it like this. I just go day by day and hope that it'll be good.

Combining RET with a creative drawing is an often used intervention of impact therapists. In a sense, the drawing disputes the client's irrational belief that there is reason to hope that things are getting better. Ratings, lists, boxes, or circles are often used in Impact Therapy. In the example below, the impact therapist drew circles to help the client see how he was misperceiving reality.

Example

Counselor: Let me draw something for you, and then I want us to discuss which one accurately portrays your relationship.

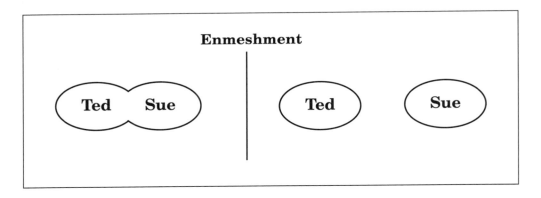

Counselor: Ted, you keep talking as if you and Sue are still connected, and yet she has told you it is over. I don't see how talking about how things are going to be in the future fits if the accurate picture of your relationship is the one on the right. Which drawing really depicts your relationship?

Client: I don't want it to be the one on the right.

Counselor: *(Using a very kind voice)* I know, but I think you know which one is true. For you to get better, you have to see yourself as separate from Sue. We can talk about how you can make it without her.

Client: I want Sue. *(Pause)* I know; Sue doesn't want me. She wants to be separate.

The impact therapist conceptualized the problem in an RET framework and used the drawings to dispute Ted's insistence that the relationship was still going on. The drawings forced the client to see the relationship in a clear, concrete way.

Another theory that the impact therapist combines with RET is Gestalt Therapy. The impact therapist often uses two chairs, one to represent the client's irrational self-talk and one to represent the client's rational self-talk.

Example

Counselor: I am going to get you to have a dialogue with yourself so that you can hear your self-talk and even try to dispute it. Sit in this seat which I've labeled "irrational," and verbalize one thought that you have that makes you feel so guilty.

Client: (*Moves to the irrational chair and then thinks for a few seconds*) It is my responsibility to make my mom happy.

Counselor: Now sit in the rational chair. What do you want to say to that part of you?

Client: (*Moves to the rational chair*) Look, she is physically and mentally ill, and she likes to wallow in self-pity. I'm not a psychiatrist or a doctor. It is not my duty to make her happy. I've done all that I can.

Counselor: (*Motions for the client to move to the irrational chair*) What is your response?

Client: I've got to take care of her. Everyone else has abandoned her. I'm all she's got left.

Counselor: Sit in the rational seat and see if you can refute that?

Client: (*Changes seats*) I can't take care of her. She needs constant help, and I have to work. I'm not abandoning her. I will do what I can, but it is now killing me to go see her every weekend. Plus, it does not help her all that much.

Counselor: Change seats.

Client: (*Client moves*) If I stop going to visit, it means I don't love her. She tells me that all the time.

Counselor: What is your response?

Client: (*Changes seats; sits for a long time*) I don't know what to say to that.

Counselor: Let me sit there, and I'll give you a rational answer. (*Moves*) Not going to see Mom has nothing to do with loving her. I do love her! It is just too draining to make that drive every weekend. I have offered for her to move here, but she refuses because she wants to be near her doctor.

Disputing irrational self-talk using two chairs is a commonly used Impact Therapy technique. The impact therapist used the combination of creative Gestalt techniques and RET to help the client verbalize the irrational sentences and see that the self-talk needs to be disputed. The impact therapist, at the end of the above example, played the rational part since the client was not able to come up with any disputing comment. Some counselors would not play the rational part, thinking that the client should come up with the disputing sentence. In Impact Therapy, the goal is to have the client change the self-talk and not to wait to see if the client can come up with good disputing sentences. There are times when the therapist will wait for the client to come up with disputing sentences; but when the client cannot, as in this example, the impact therapist will show the client rational self-talk.

There are many other ways in which impact therapists use RET. Throughout this book, there are numerous examples of the use of RET by itself or in conjunction with other theories and techniques. The impact therapist often uses RET with Transactional Analysis, which is another major theory of Impact Therapy.

Transactional Analysis and Impact Therapy

I mentioned in the section above that RET has been the most important theory that I have learned in my 30 years of being a counselor. A very close second in importance for me is Transactional Analysis (TA). TA is a theory that I believe every counselor should know because it makes interactions between people understandable. It is an essential part of Impact Therapy. (*TA Today* by Stewart and Joines [1987] is a good source for more information on TA.) TA is an excellent theory for understanding the client and the dynamics of relationships, including the counseling relationship, because it is a theory that describes human interaction and behavior in terms of different ego states.

The three main ego states are the **Parent**, the **Adult**, and the **Child**. The Parent is divided into two parts, the **Critical Parent** and the **Nurturing Parent**. The Child is also divided into two parts, the **Okay**, **Free**, or **Natural Child** and the **Not Okay** or **Adapted Child**.

The different ego states develop during childhood. Early messages and beliefs are logged like tape recordings in the different ego states. Some of these recordings play constantly in people's heads. Many clients have very large Not Okay Child ego states that cause them to feel bad about themselves. Other clients have a large Adapted Child ego state and, thus, feel like they have to please all the time. Many of these same clients have large Critical Parents inside their heads that beat up on them with all kinds of shoulds and critical messages. Knowing that there are different ego states helps the counselor understand the client's frame of reference. That is, the impact therapist who uses TA is always thinking about what ego state the client is in.

Everyone interacts from these different ego states and most usually has one or two that dominate. The ideal healthy person comes from either the Adult, Free Child, or Nurturing Parent. However, most clients are dominated by some ego state other than the Adult. The impact therapist who uses TA tries to determine the ego state of her client by observing the voice pattern, body language, and the client's words.

Briefly, the **Critical Parent** ego state is recognized by a biting, condescending, or punitive voice tone. Also indicative of the Critical Parent is finger pointing, arms folded with chin set, eyes rolling upward with disgust, and words like "should," "must," "don't," and "never."

The **Nurturing Parent** is a positive part of one's personality and, unfortunately, is often underdeveloped because it was not modeled at home. Many people cannot nurture themselves, so they look for others to do it. Nurturing gestures include a consoling touch, a pat on the back, a smile, and/or caring looks. The tone of voice is supportive, caring, warm, and encouraging; and the words to look for are "you can do it," "I'll help you," and "I love you."

The **Adult** ego state is the part that thinks. It is the computer part of the personality. Ideally, a person has a large Adult since the Adult part is the thinking part. A person in her Adult ego state is relaxed and unhurried. This person makes good eye contact and talks in a calm, direct, self-assured voice. The Adult uses words like "let's talk," "it's unfortunate," "let me think about this."

The **Okay** or **Free Child** is the part of the personality that feels good about herself and likes to have fun. This part enjoys life and is the ego state that laughs, smiles, and plays. The Free Child is curious and gets excited when doing new things.

The **Not Okay Child** is the ego state that exhibits feeling bad about one's self. Feelings of low self-esteem, worthlessness, and not being good enough are all located in the Not Okay Child. Gestures and body language include slumping of the shoulders, squirming, pouting, and looking down or away. The voice may be sullen, whining, fast, and loud or scared with phrases like "I'm worthless," "I'm no good," "I can't do anything right."

The **Not Okay Child** is seen as the **Adapted Child** when the person has a strong desire to please others so he adapts to others' wishes. This part is always trying to win approval from someone by constantly trying to live up to someone else's expectations. This part does not think but rather takes his cues from others.

Impact therapists use TA in a variety of different ways. The therapist teaches the client TA and then uses it with the client to help him understand why he has the problems he has. The other way TA is used is in observing the ego state of the client throughout the session. An impact therapist uses TA immediately upon meeting the client in that she is always alert to what ego state the client is in. The therapist is also aware when the client shifts ego states during the session. TA gives the impact therapist a good map for understanding clients during the session and for comprehending how clients interact with others in their daily lives. Impact Therapy is built upon Adult to Adult interactions in that the therapist tries hard to access the client's Adult ego state. When a client is really hurting due to something that happened or some self-disclosure, the impact therapist will see the value in using her own Nurturing Parent to show support for the client.

The impact therapist does elicit feelings from the client but also spends much time getting the client to think (Adult) about what he is doing and how he makes himself feel the way that he does. **Impact Therapy is built on the idea that a person can change if he can strengthen his Adult ego state.** Adult strengthening is accomplished by heightening a client's awareness of his ego states and then helping him develop his Adult. Adult strengthening takes place when the client learns how to use RET to challenge the Parent and Child ego states.

Impact therapists use TA in many different ways in the session to help the client understand his interactions. The impact therapist will explain the basics of TA and then discuss which ego state or states the client is in regarding the given problem. Very often, the impact therapist will draw the different ego states of the client and, if it is an interaction problem, the person with whom the client is having the problem. Clients find it very helpful to see visually their interaction patterns. Often, the ego states are drawn according to size and situation.

The following example shows one way the impact therapist uses TA. The therapist integrates TA with some creative techniques and RET to help the client.

Example

Counselor: (*Having taught the basics of TA during the last session*) Let me try to show you what is going on with you and your mom. When your mom, who was drunk, came into your room, you were in your Adult studying for your history test; but your Child enlarged as your mom started getting on you about being lazy, stupid, and not caring. Your Child ended up quite large, and your Adult quite small. Here's how that looks.

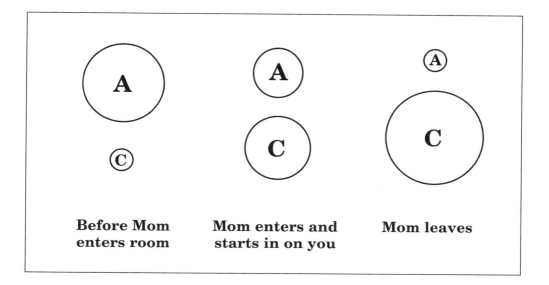

| Before Mom enters room | Mom enters and starts in on you | Mom leaves |

Counselor: Is this accurate as to what happens to you?

Client: That's exactly what happens. I don't know how to avoid going to my Child when she attacks me. She says such hurtful things.

Counselor: You're right. She does. The key for you is to deflect those thoughts by using your Adult shield. When she comes in, you need to think to yourself, "Mom is drunk. She doesn't know what she is saying. This has to do with her and not me." Inez, you have to use your Adult because your Child is under attack by your mom's Critical Parent. Here's how it could look.

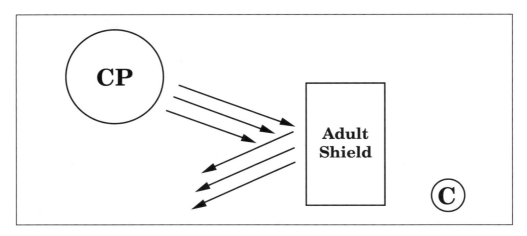

Client: What is my Adult shield?

Counselor: It is your Adult realizing that your mom is an alcoholic, and alcoholics often say cruel, insensitive things that are not at all true. Here, take this shield. (*Hands client a 12 x 12 piece of Plexiglass*) When comments come at you, your Adult says, "Protect yourself." (*Tries to poke client; client lifts the shield and blocks the counselor's hand.*) That's it. You kept me from getting to you. Your shield is your understanding that your mom is an alcoholic. Your shield is self-talk that goes something like this: "There goes Mom saying those things again. This has nothing to do with me." If you use your shield, you can deflect her critical comments and keep yourself from activating the Not Okay Child.

Client: You're saying not to listen to her.

Counselor: What she is saying is not true. It is the alcohol talking. I would say do not listen to her when she is drunk, and maybe not listen to her when she is sober. You always need to keep this shield handy or else you will find yourself going to your Child. Here's a question for you. Even though you are only 14, who has more Adult, you or your mom?

Client: (*Thinks for a minute*) I think I see your point. I probably have more Adult, and that's sad. I want her to be the adult and the parent, and most of the time I end up doing it.

Counselor: Does all this TA stuff help?

Client: A lot! I understand what is going on. Before it was just chaos. Now all I have to do is stay in my Adult—I have to remember to use my shield.

In this example the impact therapist, wanting the client to hear about, see, and experience the different ego states, integrated TA with creative techniques of drawings, the shield, and the simulated poking. TA drawings are used frequently in Impact Therapy because often clients gain more from seeing than hearing. The impact therapist does all kinds of drawings such as using different sized ego states (drawings 1 and 2 below), the Parent and Child squeezing out the Adult ego state (3, top part) and the Adult being free to communicate (3, bottom part), and the Parent and Child overlapping the Adult (4, below). Another very helpful drawing is the Ego Gram that depicts the different ego states in a bar graph (5, below). Clients often take the drawings home to remind them of what is happening in their lives.

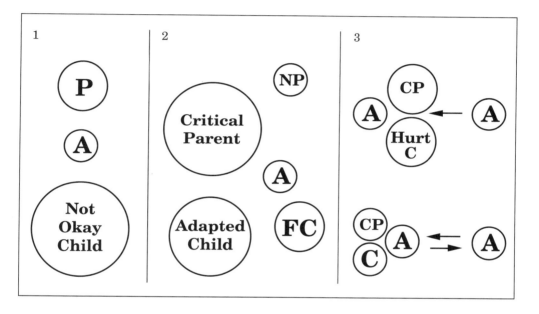

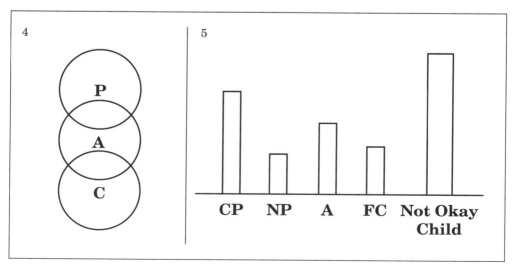

If I had to pick the most useful and helpful prop in Impact Therapy, it would be a small child's chair, used to represent the Child ego state. The effect of pulling up a small chair and having clients either look at it or sit in it when discussing their Child ego state is often quite profound. The Child becomes real to them, and they very quickly experience the feelings of their Child, especially when they sit in the chair.

Example

Client: I get so upset when I see her talking to someone. I do all kinds of things to get her out of the situation. I have faked being sick; I have thrown a temper tantrum; I have grabbed her; and I have totally interrupted the conversation. I can't help myself.

Counselor: That's not true. Ron, it's the little boy that gets scared. (*Pulls up small chair*) It sounds like if you don't learn to control him, she will leave. She said that when I saw the two of you last week; and yet on Saturday, the scared little guy went wild again.

Client: (*Staring at the chair*) I've never felt secure about relationships. When I was 5, Mom kept leaving and coming back. She left us with my grandmother once, then with Uncle Dave, and then with Aunt Peggy.

Counselor: (*Knowing that Ron's wife is going to leave if something does not change immediately, uses a warm, but firm voice*) Your feelings about someone leaving you when you were young were real, but that was at least 25 years ago. That was then, and this is now. We cannot do anything about then, but we can do something about now; and if we don't do something real soon, your wife will most likely leave you. When you relate to your wife, are you in the Adult (*pulls up a regular sized chair*) or in the Child?

Client: The Child.

Counselor: Our counseling needs to be about your staying out of the little boy chair. (*Using RET with TA*) Ron, what do you tell yourself that causes you to be in the Child's chair?

Client: I know she will leave me. I'm not enough for her! She's going to find someone who is smarter or richer than I am. I can't live without her. I think about this all the time.

Counselor:	I know, and Kellie is getting tired of it, especially since it is getting worse. We need to start talking about very specific things you can do to change. Sit over in the Adult chair. (*Client moves.*) How would an Adult handle the situation where your wife is talking to someone?
Client:	I'd have to think something different, I guess.
Counselor:	That is exactly right. I want us to take a look at the things the Child says to himself, and I'm going to help the Adult challenge the Child's negative, self-defeating thinking.

In this example, the impact therapist used the small chair to help the client see that he needs to get to his Adult. The example ended with the therapist starting to use RET to help the client strengthen his Adult. Throughout the book, there are numerous examples using the small chair, the Adult chair, and the Parent chair which is often created by the counselor standing on the chair. To dramatize certain interactions, I often stand on a chair to represent the Parent ego state of the client or the Parent ego state of someone with whom the client is interacting, while the client sits in the Child's chair and looks up at the Parent.

Gestalt Therapy and Impact Therapy

A major premise in Gestalt Therapy is to heighten the awareness of the client. This is accomplished quite often in Gestalt Therapy by using an empty chair to bring the problem into the present. The impact therapist very much agrees with this premise and, therefore, has a variety of ways to bring about awareness. Impact Therapy also uses the powerful technique of talking to an empty chair to get the client in touch with her feelings or thoughts about a situation. The technique of standing in the chair (as described above) definitely heightens the client's awareness of whom she puts above her and how she feels in the Child chair. The impact therapist will also use various movement activities, such as having the client stand and move forward while the counselor pulls on her arm. This helps the client experience being held back.

Example

Counselor: I want us to stand up. (*Both stand.*) Give me your arm. Now I want you to try to go forward and experience being held back. Think about what and who is holding you back.

Another major emphasis in both Gestalt Therapy and Impact Therapy is helping clients finish their "unfinished business." Gestalt Therapy emphasizes going deep on the Depth Chart as does Impact Therapy. Gestalt therapists and impact therapists are not afraid to get clients into their unfinished business that often centers around their family of origin, sex, shame, or abandonment. Very often impact occurs when the client gets to work through deep-seated emotions which are due to some event that happened weeks, months, or years ago.

The impact therapist most often uses Gestalt Therapy to get the client in touch with her feelings. He then uses other theories (usually TA and RET) to help the client understand and reframe the situation. In the example below, the impact therapist uses Gestalt Therapy and other theories and techniques to focus and funnel the session.

Example

Client: I am afraid of my dad. I don't know why. He used to spend a lot of time with me. We went fishing, and I love to fish. I would fish anytime, but now I...

Counselor: (*Interrupts the client with a soft, firm voice*) Wait a minute. Let's find out why you are afraid of your dad. (*Using Gestalt Therapy, pulls up an empty chair and stands on the chair, representing Dad*) What would you say to your dad if he were here?

Client: (*Stares at chair; looks up at Dad sheepishly*) Dad, why don't you approve of anything I do? Ever since I quit football, you have treated me differently. So you were a star. Dad, I can't be a star football player. Why can't you love me for who I am?

Counselor: Have you ever said any of these things to your dad?

Client: No, I couldn't do that.

Counselor: Why not?

Client: Because I don't know what he would do.

Counselor: (*Getting down from chair*) Sit over here in Dad's chair and respond.

Client: (*Moves and stares at his chair*) I don't know if he would be mad, hurt, or concerned. I truly don't know what he would say.

Counselor: Move back to your seat. (*Using RET*) Let's talk about what you tell yourself that prevents you from talking to your dad?

Client: I am afraid.

Counselor: Are you afraid of what he will do, such as hit you; or are you afraid of what he'll say or think?

Client: I'm afraid that he'll be disappointed.

Counselor: But you just said you don't know what he would feel. You tell yourself something like "If I tell Dad my feelings, he'll be upset, and that would be awful!" But you did say he may not be upset but rather concerned for you. Is

	what keeps you from talking to him that you're thinking the worst and then telling yourself you couldn't stand it.
Client:	I guess so.
Counselor:	Let's look more into your self-talk and see if it is true or not.

The counselor combined Gestalt with RET to focus and funnel the session. The counselor saw that the client needed to clarify what he was afraid of and then to come to understand how he causes that fear.

Additional Examples of Theoretical Integration of Impact Therapy

There will be times when the impact therapist uses a theory such as RET, TA, or Reality Therapy by itself and other times when theories are combined and creative techniques are also used. It is important to note how the counselor focuses the session rather than lets the client go on with stories. In the first example, the therapist wants the session to have impact and sees where teaching RET would be very beneficial.

Example 1

Client:	...and let me tell you what else they said. They said
Counselor:	(*Seeking to focus the session*) Libby, I am going to stop you because it is not so important that I hear what they said. It is much more important for us to take a look at what you are telling yourself about what they said. I want to write down your self-talk so that you can see exactly what you are telling yourself.
Client:	What do you mean, my self-talk? Are you saying that I talk to myself?!
Counselor:	(*In a calm voice*) We all talk to ourselves, but often we don't know it. I do, you do, everybody does. Let me show you this ABC model that helps in understanding where our feelings come from and how our self-talk plays a big part in how we feel. (*Goes to wipe board and starts writing*) The A is the event which was being at the reunion and people were talking about you. C is the feeling which was anger. B is your self-talk about A. That's what I want us to look at.

In this example, the impact therapist interrupts the client in order to focus the client. She used her voice, writing, theory, and teaching in hopes of helping the client better understand her anger when she was at the reunion.

Example 2

In this example, the impact therapist uses Reality Therapy to get a contract and to focus the session.

Client: I just couldn't take it any more, so I went into the back room and called him; and wouldn't you know it, Mom came in and caught me talking to him. Then all hell broke loose.

Counselor: (*Using Reality Therapy*) Let's go back to what it is that you want.

Client: I don't know. Why can't they leave me alone and let me date who I want to?

Counselor: What is it that you want?

Client: For them to trust me!

Counselor: Is what you're doing getting you what you want?

Client: No, it is not.

Counselor: If you are clear that you want them to trust you and what you are doing is not working, I think we should talk about a plan that gets you what you want. I want us to write out your plan so that when we are finished, you can copy it and have it to follow when you are at home.

Knowing theory cannot be overemphasized; the impact therapist has to be knowledgeable in a number of theories and comfortable combining them when it is helpful for the client.

TIMING

Proper timing is crucial in counseling. There are definitely instances when the counselor wants to go slow, go fast, focus the session on a different topic, or focus and funnel the session to a deeper level. Moving too quickly or too slowly can hinder, even destroy, the counseling. The impact therapist pays attention to timing because he knows that, while he wants to have impact during the session, he does not want to be abrupt or insensitive. If the use of creative techniques or theory is poorly timed, the client may become annoyed due to her lack of readiness to deal with the issue.

Letting topics or issues pass when they could be focused and funneled is another mistake in timing that I notice when I supervise practice sessions during my classes or workshops. There are times when the therapist will want to avoid "heavy" issues and times when the therapist will want to try to push the client deeper into the issue.

One of the best ways for any therapist to know if the timing is right is to watch the client carefully as she tries some technique or strategy. Usually there will be a reaction that lets the therapist know if the timing is off. Often, counselors are so worried about their intervention, they fail to observe the client. Counselors, at times, see painful reactions and automatically back off, which is not always the best thing to do. The counselor who has a good sense of timing will appropriately take the client deeper into the pain rather than backing away or letting the client back away.

It is impossible to give specific guidelines about how to time focusing and funneling since timing is so individualized. However, proper timing is crucial. One additional way for the therapist to check his timing is for him to simply ask the client if this would be a good time to explore a certain issue.

Poor Timing

Example 1

It is 10 minutes into the first session.

Client: I'm not sure about you or this counseling stuff. I've got lots inside, but I don't know. My dad made me come. Boy, do I hate that man.

Counselor: Let's do this. I want you to look at this empty chair and imagine your dad is sitting here. What would you say to him?

Client: What are you talking about? I'm not going to talk to no empty chair.

Counselor: But you seem angry at your dad.

Client: I don't even know if I want to talk to you, and I'm sure not going to let you tell people that I talked to an empty chair.

The therapist accurately assessed the client's need to work on his issues with his dad, but the timing was poor, given the client had just mentioned how he still was not sure about being there for counseling. Mistakenly, the counselor tried to focus the session before working through the rapport and contract phases.

Example 2

Client: I don't like my new school. I loved my other school. It was small, and I knew everyone. This school really scares me. That's why I fake being sick, because there are days I just dread going to school. Riding to school is okay. I am on the bus for 30 minutes. Last week we saw two deer. One day we saw a fox. Maybe I'll grow up and work at a zoo. What does one have to do to work at a zoo?

Counselor: I am not sure, but I'll look into it for you. Why do you think you would like to work in a zoo?

Client: I like all kinds of animals. I watch all those shows on television about animals. I saw one last week about elephants. They showed....

Counselor: (*After about 3 minutes of listening to stories about elephants*) Can we come back to the school issue?

Client: Let me tell you about this one other show. It was on monkeys. It was real interesting about all the different kinds of monkeys. They had segments from....

The counselor waited too long to focus. His timing was poor, and he missed an opportunity to focus and funnel when he asked about working at a zoo instead of focusing the session around the issue of her not liking her new school and faking being sick.

Good Timing

Example 1

Client: I just feel so bad for my dad—that he has to put up with her. (*Starts to tear up*) She is a sick lady—very abusive and negative. (*In a story voice*) Last week she was taking me to the store for some Christmas shopping, and we had the biggest fight.

Counselor: (*Realizes that the tears may have been important and does not want to miss the opportunity to focus and funnel the session; using a soft, empathetic voice*) Connie, what were the tears about? They seem important.

Client: My dad. He's the most important person in the world to me, and he's dying of liver cancer. I think about it all the time, but he told me not to tell anyone. He's a very private person.

Counselor: (*Using a warm, nurturing voice*) I am sorry to hear that about your dad. I think it is good for you to talk to someone about such a painful thing. Tell me some more about your dad and your feelings.

Client: (*Sobbing*) They say he has less than 6 months to live. Last night we talked and....

The counselor, who is always thinking about trying to focus and funnel in order to have impact, made the decision to switch from talking about her mom to whatever was causing the tears. The tears seemed important. The client was telling a story that did not seem to be too important. Too often, counselors just follow the client's stories that lead nowhere, whereas the impact therapist sees that a timely interruption provides opportunity to have an impact.

Example 2

Client: (*In a very negative, angry tone*) I don't know why I am here. It is the judge's fault. She is out to get me.

Counselor: (*Decides not to mention the shoplifting and the hitting of the policewoman*) Let's not talk about why you are here. Let's talk about how your life is going.

Client: (*In a very angry voice*) My life is fine, just fine. I don't like living with my aunt and uncle.

Counselor: (*Decides to ignore the angry voice; also knows the client's mom is in jail for murder but is not sure if the client is ready to talk about it; using a calm voice*) We can talk about living with relatives, or we can talk about anything you want to talk about. Music, friends, school— anything is fine with me.

Client: I like my friends. We are all into music. We are trying to get a group going. We practice twice a week over at Dale's house. I play the guitar.

Counselor: (*Trying to build rapport and realizing that the client is not yet ready to talk about anything related to his arrest*) That's great. How long have you been doing this?

Client: Nearly a year.

Counselor: What kind of music are you playing?

In this example, the counselor could sense that the girl would probably not talk if he tried to focus on some relevant issues, so he just threw out a variety of topics. Aware of proper timing, he knew the most important thing was to build rapport and not sound too much like a counselor.

TEACHING

Teaching is an integral part of Impact Therapy. An impact therapist realizes that there are times when teaching is necessary. Unfortunately, many training programs are usually critical of this aspect of therapy and advocate that teaching should not be part of a counseling session. In my years of practice, I have found that teaching definitely is necessary. Usually, teaching is not the primary function of the counselor, but it is a helpful counseling activity. A good therapist should not feel that it is wrong to spend time providing needed information to a client. An impact therapist may find herself teaching such subjects as where feelings come from, how to live a more balanced life, how to have fun, how and where to meet people, the effects of alcohol on family members, stress management, sexual practices, birth control, good grooming, parenting, menopause, diet, exercise, and many other topics.

It is important to realize that teaching needs to be properly timed, well thought out, and delivered in such a way that the client gains useful information. Beginning counselors either never teach or mistakenly teach ineffectively by lecturing or turning the session almost into a classroom situation. The examples below illustrate how impact therapists use teaching in their sessions.

Example 1

Client: I've never had a real job, just odd jobs. Before going into treatment, I was drunk more than I was sober. This is the longest I've been sober since I was 15. I don't really know how to get a job.

Counselor: I think I can help you by giving you some information about how to go about finding a job. There are a number of things you can do, and it is good to do all of them because you never know which one will lead you to a job. One of the best things to do is to get clear as to what kinds of jobs you are looking for and then start checking the paper and potential employers for openings. Do you know what kinds of jobs you want?

Client: Well, not really. How do I figure that out?

Counselor: Let me tell you a little bit about how to figure that out.

The counselor sees that the client has very limited knowledge regarding how to find a job, so she decides to teach him. She figures time will be much better spent teaching than waiting for the client to figure it out; also, the real impact for this client is finding a job and not figuring out how to find a job.

Example 2

Client: I have no idea where to meet people, much less how to meet them.

Counselor: Let me give you some ideas of where to meet people. You can meet people anywhere—in the grocery store, church, library, when taking a walk, in restaurants, bars, and hundreds of other places.

Client: I've never thought about meeting people in the library or on a walk or in the grocery store. How do you do that?

Counselor: You start up a conversation by making a comment or asking a question.

Client: How do I do that?

Counselor: I will teach you some ways, and then we'll practice. In order for you to change your life, you do need to start meeting people. I'm willing to teach you if, between now and our next session, you are willing to try out what you learned.

Client: I don't know. It sounds scary to me.

Counselor: That's understandable. Many people scare themselves when they try new things. Let's first talk about what to say and how to say it, and then we'll take a look at how you can reduce your fear by changing the self-talk in your head.

The counselor saw that the client had lived a very shy, sheltered life and decided to teach her about meeting people. He also realized that he would need to help her with her fears, but he stayed focused on the topic of meeting people, instead of mixing the two topics of meeting people and the fears. He wanted to teach more about meeting people; then he will teach RET and how she can dispute her negative self-talk.

Example 3

Counselor: It is apparent that you and your brother fight a lot, and you don't like it.

Client: No, I hate it.

Counselor: Let me show you a model that can help you understand the interaction between you and your brother. Have you ever been taught Transactional Analysis, also called TA?

Client: No, I don't think so.

Counselor: Inside of each of us are three parts, or ego states. Let me draw them here for you, and then I'll tell you about each one. The three parts are Parent, Adult, and Child....

The counselor would spend 5 to 10 minutes teaching the main tenets of TA, using the situation that she had just been describing.

Example 4

Counselor: It is seems to me that you have no idea where your feelings come from. I think I'll spend a few minutes teaching you a theory about how we cause our feelings by what we tell ourselves. This seems to be a good place to start since you said that you do not have a clue as to why you feel the way you do. Once I go through the theory, we'll take a look at some of those feelings you were talking about. The model I am going to show you is an ABC model....

The counselor would spend 5 to 10 minutes teaching the main tenets of RET, interacting with the client and using examples from her life.

TRAINING

The impact therapist understands that counseling often involves training. By training, I mean helping clients learn new skills by having them practice and receive feedback. The impact therapist realizes that there will be times when she will decide to train the client in how to do something better—**therapy involves coaching.** The reason for this is many times clients have little or no experience or understanding of how to go about making changes that would be valuable in their lives. Assertiveness training, job interviewing, talking with parents, and meeting new people are all forms of training in which a therapist may engage. Two other forms of training that are very important are how to be nurturing to oneself and others and how to think or use the Adult ego state. Clients often do not know how to be kind to themselves since they have had no modeling of that behavior, nor do they know how to think for themselves because they have always relied on someone else to think for them.

Training in a session often takes on a different look than most counseling sessions. The sessions often include discussion, then role playing or practice, followed by feedback. After the feedback, there is more practicing and additional feedback. The emphasis is on learning a new behavior or skill. When a client is being trained, the session may be in steps, with mastering one skill, then moving to the next skill. Often, training is coupled with more in-depth exploration since many times a client's negative self-talk or Parent or Child ego state gets in the way of mastering new behaviors.

The following examples illustrate how impact therapists use training in their sessions.

Example 1

Client: I don't know how to meet people. I have always been very shy.

Counselor: Mazy, I think what would be helpful is to have you practice with me right now. Let's say you are at the dance, and you are going to initiate a conversation with a boy.

Client: I don't know what to say.

Counselor: Let's stand up. We'll pretend we are standing at the punch bowl. What could you say?

Client: Honest, I don't know what I'd say. This is too hard.

Counselor: Wait a minute. Did you ever learn something that at first seemed impossible?

Client: Skiing. I was ready to quit, but my brother kept on encouraging me, and now I am a better skier than he is.

Counselor: (*Impact therapists see the value in using analogies.*) Let's look at this like skiing. No one starts on the advanced slopes, and most start on the bunny slope. Usually it is awkward for the first day or so, but after seeing others ski plus trying it themselves, most people get the hang of it. Almost everyone gets it if they don't give up and keep practicing. That's what we are going to do—practice. Tell you what. I'll be you, and you be the boy....

In this example, the impact counselor saw that training was necessary. Also, by the counselor's using an analogy, the client seemed to get a better grasp of the idea of learning something new. The counselor would spend as much time as necessary helping the girl learn how to meet people at dances and other places.

Example 2

Client: I never say nice things to myself. I criticize myself all the time.

Counselor: (*Stands on chair in front of client as client looks up*) So you have this huge Critical Parent in your head that beats on you all the time; and your Nurturing Parent, the part of you that is nice and says kind things to you, is very small (*now sits on floor with head slumped down*).

Client:	(*Staring at the counselor slumped on the floor*) That's right. I do not know how to nurture myself.
Counselor:	I want us to practice using the nurturing part of you. Let's take the incident of the not having money after getting gas. You said you beat up on yourself for days for being so stupid. What could the nurturing part of you have said?
Client:	I don't know.
Counselor:	Think about it. What could you have said?
Client:	(*Using a cold voice*) You made a mistake. So what.
Counselor:	You're on the right track, but your voice was harsh, and your comments could have been more gentle. What about saying (using a soft, nurturing voice), "You made a mistake. The lady trusted you to go get the money. It's no big deal. Everyone makes mistakes."
Client:	Nobody has ever talked to me that way.
Counselor:	What I am trying to do is to get you to talk to yourself in a kind and encouraging way. Everyone needs nurturing, and everyone can nurture themselves. Now you practice being kind to you. Let's go to that incident the other day on the computer. What could you have said when you tried to learn that new computer program?
Client:	You mean instead of "You're stupid. You can't learn anything!"
Counselor:	That's the huge critical part that's on the chair. What could the nurturing part say?

The impact therapist, using TA theory and the creative techniques of standing on the chair and sitting on the floor, emphasized the need for the client to develop the ability to nurture herself. The counselor realized that much training would be needed because the client had experienced very little nurturing in her life.

THINKING

Thinking is an essential part of Impact Therapy. I list it as one of the five **T**s because not enough emphasis is put on the value of thinking. Many counseling training programs emphasize listening to such a degree that counselors spend their time in sessions mostly listening and rarely thinking. Too often, the counselor simply asks a question or offers a reflection based on the last thing the client said. **The impact therapist is not only busy listening but also is busy thinking strategy, theory, and creative possibilities.**

Not only do I believe that the counselor has to think, but also that the client needs to think. Many therapists focus almost entirely on getting clients to express their feelings. There are therapists who are doing healing work of different kinds, and they only emphasize feelings. Talking about or experiencing feelings alone does not usually bring about change. Getting clients to think about their feelings, the circumstances that led up to the feelings, and the self-talk involved with the feelings can be instrumental in helping clients understand and possibly change their feelings. The impact therapist focuses on both the feelings and thoughts of the client and is aware of the importance of getting the client to think differently about his situation. By the therapist's making the counseling clear and concrete, the client usually spends a good portion of the session thinking about what he is saying and what the counselor is pointing out through the use of theory or some creative technique.

Therapists using theories such as RET, TA, and Reality Therapy understand the importance of thinking along with feelings. I realize that some sessions may require most of the time to be spent allowing the client to get in touch with and explore his feelings, but I am always considering whether or not getting the client to think may have more impact, especially after using some creative or Gestalt technique to get him deeply in touch with his feelings. Following are examples showing how the impact therapist thinks and how he gets the client to think during a session.

Example 1

Client: ...so I just don't know what I should do. The whole thing is a mess. I can't seem to get a grip on anything. My doctor has said that I have got to get some rest, but I feel that I have to be with my baby. And then there's the issue of do I move the baby to another hospital because of all the feelings I have?

Counselor: (*Who has been thinking while John has been more or less repeating himself*) John, I believe I have the picture, but I want to think about this since it is so complex. (*Pause*) I realize that there are many different issues, your health, the baby's health, the hospital's negligence, and your father's position at the hospital. It seems to me that we should talk first about your health; then we'll take a look at the other issues. We have got to do what it takes to get you healthy; then you can look at some of these other decisions.

This is an example of when the counselor takes time to think about what has been said. The counselor felt that he needed to take a minute to process all the aspects of the client's problem in order to come up with the best way to approach the problem.

Example 2

It is 25 minutes into a scheduled 1-hour session.

Client: I just want some relief. I can't stand the marriage any more, but I can't throw away 19 years of marriage. I know it is bad for me and my son, but he won't move out, so I am stuck. I have so many feelings about the divorce. I have such anger.

Counselor: (*Using Reality Therapy to get her to think*) What is it that you want for yourself?

Client: I don't know.

Counselor: What is it that you want?

Client: To feel better about my life.

Counselor: Is what you're doing working?

Client: (*Thinks for a few seconds*) No, it is definitely not.

Counselor: Do you think you need a new plan in order to get what you want?

Client: When you put it that way, I can see that I do.

Counselor: What new things do you need to do in order to get what you want?

Client: I have to let myself think about divorce and not cross it off the list of options. I am miserable, and I do want to feel better. I have a lot of living left since I'm not even 40. I can't let him define who I am. Also, I do have to let go of the memories of how it was when we first met.

Counselor: I want you to think for a minute. If you were to rate your life on a 1-10 scale with 10 being great, what would you give your life?

Client: A 4 at best.

Counselor: If you were free of your husband, what do you think your life would be?

Client: It'd be a 6 at least. I look forward to the times he goes away on business.

Counselor: It'd be a 6 with the possibility of it going to an 8, 9, or even a 10. What is the highest your life can go now?

Client:	As long as I am married, it can't get any higher than a 5 because of his crazy ideas of what he wants from a wife.
Counselor:	Think about what you are saying. Your life gets better if you leave him and has potential of being really good, and you are choosing to hold on to a 4. Can you explain that to me?
Client:	(*Pauses*) No. It doesn't make any sense. It would be scary to get divorced.

In this example the impact therapist used Reality Therapy which is an excellent theory for getting clients to think because the counselor asks many questions. The client definitely has to think in order to answer the kinds of questions that come from a Reality Therapy point of view. The therapist then used the rating scale which also made the client think. Much of Impact Therapy involves both the client and the counselor thinking through the problem or situation that is causing trouble.

Example 3

Counselor:	Martina, I'm going to use two chairs for us to look at your situation. Come sit in this small chair and be the girl that is feeling bad. What does she say to herself?
Client:	(*Eyes down, crying softly*) It's my fault they got divorced. I should have been able to keep them from fighting. I want a mommy and daddy.
Counselor:	(*Using a kind, but strong voice*) Now sit in this chair. This is your thinking chair. (*Client moves.*) Look at that small chair and respond to what that part just said. (*Client stares at the chair.*) How old are you?
Client:	10.
Counselor:	How old are your mom and dad?
Client:	Dad is 30, and Mom is 27.
Counselor:	I'd like you to explain to the little girl, using your thinking part, why it is not your fault.
Client:	(*Thinks for a minute*) They got married when they were real young. They are very different.
Counselor:	Do you think 10 year olds can cause parents to get divorced?
Client:	Some maybe can, but I am a pretty good kid. I don't cause much trouble. They are getting divorced because they don't like each other very much.

Counselor:	What about what the little girl said about wanting a mom and a dad?
Client:	They still are going to be my mom and dad. They just aren't going to live together. You know what, it's probably better. They won't fight as much. I'm glad we're all going to be in the same town. In fact, Dad is living only five blocks from Mom.
Counselor:	Are you feeling better?
Client:	A whole lot. Thanks for helping me.
Counselor:	Your thinking part did most of the helping. Here's a pass to get back to class.

The impact counselor chose to focus on thinking by having the child move to the Adult chair instead of focusing on the crying from the Child chair. He asked Martina her age and the age of her parents to get her into her Adult in that she had to think to answer those questions. He then had her use her Adult (which is the thinking part) to respond to the Child regarding her parents and their divorce. In the end, by getting the client to think, the counselor helped her feel better about her situation.

SUMMARY

Five key concepts in Impact Therapy are **theory**, **timing**, **teaching**, **training**, and **thinking**. Impact Therapy is built on the premise that all sessions should be theory driven. Most theories are compatible with Impact Therapy although certain ones, such as Person-Centered Therapy and Psychoanalysis, are not. Since Impact Therapy is an active form of therapy, the therapist has to always be aware of the timing of her strategies and techniques. There are times during counseling when teaching and training are appropriate ways to have impact, and in most sessions, some teaching or training takes place. Thinking plays a major part in Impact Therapy, in regards to both the counselor and the client.

Chapter 3

Ways To Have Impact

I chose the name Impact Therapy because I wanted to emphasize that counselors should be trying to have some kind of impact during any counseling session. I have been asked if impact means crying or some cathartic experience. The answer is "no" because therapy can be impactful in different ways, not just in emotional outpouring. Many times, getting the client to think differently or learn something is very beneficial. In this chapter, I discuss different ways to have impact because a therapist needs to have a sense of the many options available when working with any client.

It is important to remember that no matter which of these ways the therapist uses, she will want to try to take the session to a depth level of **7** or below. Some of the paths are similar, but there are subtle differences, so I list each path separately to give more understanding of the options available when conducting therapy sessions.

In the examples below, I illustrate the many different ways to have impact. I purposely have made the examples brief since, in later chapters, I provide numerous detailed examples where I illustrate focusing and funneling.

HELP CLIENT CLARIFY

Many times in counseling, it is helpful to get the client to clarify whatever it is she is confused about. This can be very beneficial, and the counselor needs to be aware that helping a client get greater clarity about a situation is definitely a way to have impact.

Example

Client: I'm confused about what is going on with my friends. I don't know if they don't like me, are mad at me, or are just doing things that I don't enjoy. They know I don't like kickball. I am so confused; I think about this constantly.

Counselor: Why don't you tell me more, and I will try to help you clarify what is going on. I'm sure that I can get this clearer for you. Let's list the possibilities. (*To help make the session clear and concrete, stands and goes to a large* *flip chart in his office.*) Give me the first names of these friends you are talking about, and we'll list each one and why you think that person is acting the way he or she is. (*The counselor then spends the next few minutes trying to help the client get a clearer picture of what is going on.*)

HELP CLIENT INCREASE UNDERSTANDING AND AWARENESS

Helping clients understand why they do what they do can be very impactful. Greater awareness of an issue almost always is helpful for the client if she wants to change some behavior.

Example

Counselor: Let's look at how not being able to read has affected you. Do you feel equal to others?

Client: No, not really. I know when I get around those in the best reading group, I feel bad. I avoid that situation as much as possible, but the teacher seems to always put me in groups with some of them. I have always hated group work.

Counselor: Did you ever connect disliking small groups to your not being able to read?

Client: No, I don't think I thought the two were connected.

Counselor: How about your brother and sister—do you feel equal to them?

Client: I do in some things, but I guess I always think they are smarter than me because they can read.

Counselor: So you have the belief that almost everyone is better or smarter than you because almost everyone can read.

Client: Yes, that's how I have always felt, ever since the 3rd grade.

Counselor: Let's look specifically at what you are telling yourself about not being able to read. I don't know if you realize it or not, but you have many untrue and negative sentences that you run through your head about not being able to read. Can you read if I tell you what I am writing?

Client: Oh yes. I can read some, and if I know what is being written, I can remember. I have a good mind.

Counselor: I can see that. (*Stands and goes to wipe board*) Let's write some of your thoughts down and then see how true they are.

HELP CLIENT DISCOVER

In the previous example, the client gained greater understanding about something he already knew was affecting him in some ways, whereas in this example, the client discovers something that she did not know. Often clients are not aware of their feelings; and by the therapist's focusing the session and funneling it below **7**, clients discover new things about themselves.

Example

Client: I don't know why I let him do that to me.

Counselor: Roxy, would you like to figure it out?

Client: Sure, but I can't for the life of me understand why I am strong at work and then a mouse and doormat at home.

Counselor: How did your dad treat your mom?

Client: Mom saw him as king and master. She used to tell us girls that no matter what, we should always treat Daddy nice and never upset him.

Counselor: Well, wait. That seems important. What messages did you get about how a woman should let a man treat her?

Client: I never thought that my parents' relationship had that much influence on me.

Counselor: I think we need to explore this in much greater detail. (*Pulls up a small chair and places a cassette tape in the chair; client stares at the chair and tape*) When you were young, you made a tape about how a woman should treat a man. (*In a voice that says "think" rather than tell me a story*) What did you learn from your mom about how you should treat a man? What's on your tape?

Client: (*Staring at the chair and tape*) I learned a lot. I learned….

The counselor wanted the client to discover the different things she learned growing up. The use of the small chair and the tape helped emphasize the idea of tapes from childhood.

GIVE SUPPORT

Often clients need support for changes that they are going through. The impact therapist understands the necessity of being supportive when it is appropriate. In grief counseling and certain crisis situations, simply listening and being there for the client is a major way of being helpful.

Example

Client: It's still hard to believe that he's gone. It's been almost 6 months. I get lonely, and sometimes I feel scared.

Counselor: You and your husband were together for 32 years. It certainly is normal to have the feelings that you are having, especially loneliness.

Client: I thought I'd be over this by now.

Counselor: Grieving and healing take time. Let's keep talking about your feelings. It's not like you sit around all day and stare into space. You're working, going out with friends, reading. At times, you miss your husband. These are very normal parts of the grieving process.

Client:	That's helpful to hear. I have all these thoughts that run through my head about how I should be doing, about him, about the future.
Counselor:	Let's talk about some of those thoughts running through your head.

In this example, the counselor realized that this was a grief situation and knew from studying grief counseling that letting the client talk is often the best thing to do, especially if the loss was recent. I believe strongly that every counselor should take a course or do some extensive reading on grief counseling since there are so many situations where knowing grief counseling can be helpful. (*Grief Counseling and Grief Therapy* by Worden [1991], *Grief, Dying, and Death* by Rando [1984], and *Helping Children Cope With Separation and Loss* by Jewett [1994] are excellent resources for grief counseling.)

PROVIDE ENCOURAGEMENT

All people need encouragement. There will be times when encouragement can be very therapeutic and can help clients talk about or make the changes that they need.

Example

Client:	Well, I did try a couple of things you suggested this week, but I didn't do anything about getting a job. Boy, do I need a job.
Counselor:	Back up here. I am glad to hear that you tried some new things. Maybe this week we'll work on specifically trying things that may lead to a job. The main thing is you did some positive things for yourself. What things did you try?
Client:	I went for some walks. I called up two friends and got together with them. I only went to see my brother twice, and I left when he started yelling at me. That was a lot better. I never realized how going to see him gets me down.
Counselor:	This is terrific. You did a whole lot. I want to hear about all of this.
Client:	Come to think of it, this is one of the best weeks I have had in over a year. I liked walking. It does me good to get out of the house and move around. A few people even said hello to me when I passed them. It was a good week.
Counselor:	It sure sounds that way to me. You did things. I'm thrilled for you. Tell me more about this good week and how you can make this next week just as good.

DISPUTE AND HELP CLIENT DISPUTE

In my experience in the counseling profession, I have come to believe that much of what goes on in personal counseling is helping clients change their irrational beliefs. RET is built on the idea of disputing clients' irrational and self-defeating thinking. Impact Therapy expands RET to include different creative techniques, such as the use of certain props, writings, and chairs. Impact Therapy also integrates RET with TA and Gestalt Therapy in ways that make the disputing process clearer, more concrete, and more impactful.

In the example below, I show disputing as one of the Impact Therapy paths. The impact therapist is very well versed in RET and is able to use it in an effective, helpful manner.

Example

Client: ...so because I can't have children, my life is just as well as over. I think I am going to tell my husband tonight that I want a divorce. I just wish I was a complete woman!

Counselor: Wait a minute. You have said three things that I want us to take a good look at because they simply are not true. You said, "My life is over; I need a divorce, and I am not a complete woman?" Which one do you want me to dispute or help you to dispute first?

Client: They are all true. How can you say that they are not true?

Counselor: Let's look at the comment about not being a complete woman. What makes a woman complete? Are all the women who can't give birth to children incomplete?

Client: I just know that I feel incomplete.

Counselor: You feel incomplete because you tell yourself you are incomplete. The truth is that you cannot give birth to children, which has nothing to do with your being a complete woman. I want you to see that it is your thoughts that are causing your feelings, and your thoughts are not true. We'll come back to this idea, but let's look at your thought about needing a divorce. Why is that true?

Client: I feel my husband deserves to have children, and I can't give him any.

Counselor: Did he say he wanted a divorce?

Client: No, he didn't at all. He said he loved me very much, and we'd get through this.

Counselor: Does it make any sense, then, to think you need to divorce him for his benefit when says he loves you and wants to be with you?

As was mentioned in the previous chapter, the idea of disputing clients' self-talk is an essential and often used component of Impact Therapy. Many of the examples in later chapters will include different ways to dispute the client's irrational sentences.

HELP CLIENT CHOOSE

Many clients come to counseling because they are indecisive about some situation in their lives. It is often beneficial to focus the client on the options or pros and cons of a situation and then help the client make a decision as to what would be best.

Example

Client: I cannot decide whether to take the new job or not. It is a great opportunity for moving up.

Counselor: Obviously, there's something that is holding you back or at least causing you to consider not doing the job. Let's talk about why you're thinking of not taking it.

Client: Well, it means that I'll have to work some evenings and weekends. Also, it means that I will be more management rather than doing the hands on work.

Counselor: Those sound like important variables. I want us to carefully explore the pros and cons of each choice.

Client: You know the money would be great. I have thought about all the things that I could do with the extra money. The house needs some work; I could give Mom some money. I can't decide how much though. I have thought about a bunch of different options. One is to, uh,...

Counselor: (*Breaks in because she wants to focus and funnel the session*) Carlos, I think you are ahead of yourself. Before you talk all about the money, let's first focus in on the decision itself. Let's go back to the decision. (*Pulls up two chairs*) Let this chair be taking the new job and this chair staying in your current job. Sit in the one for taking the new job and talk about how it feels, both the pros and cons. One pro is money. What are other feelings and thoughts you have from this seat? (*The counselor, realizing that Carlos tends to get off track, uses the chairs to keep the client focused on the issue of the "decision" as opposed to going off in another direction.*)

HELP CLIENT STICK WITH A DECISION

Getting clients to stick with decisions which they have made during counseling is often very difficult, especially when the decision has to do with giving up an addiction of some kind. The impact therapist works hard in the session to reinforce the gains of the client and to continue to show him, through talking and other creative techniques, the positive value of his decision.

Example

Client: It has been going okay. It has now been 2 weeks, and I haven't called her or driven by her house. I've got this licked. She's history!

Counselor: But, you've done this before and then went back to her. How is this different?

Client: Oh, this is really different.

Counselor: Specifically, how. I've heard those exact words before, and then she'll call, or the two of you will run into each other, and you go back.

Client: Talking about it makes me miss her—I'd rather talk about something else.

Counselor: Well, that's exactly why we need to talk about her. It is so easy for you to say this time is different, but I don't see the strategy or the real difference between this time or any other time. (*Pulls up a small child's chair*) When you are alone, your Child part (pointing at the chair) can take over. If we talk here, I think I can coach you in how to handle that Child part, stay in your Adult (*pulls up a regular size chair*), and stay away from this defeating relationship.

Client: (*Staring at the two chairs*) You're right. I have been thinking about those good times we had. Boy, were they good. I don't think I'll ever meet anyone like her.

Counselor: With thoughts like that, how are you going to stick with your decision that you say is best for you?

GIVE PERMISSION

A session may prove very helpful for the client if she feels she now has permission to do or say something. Some therapists are taught to never offer an opinion or give permission for anything. Clients often feel doing certain things would be wrong when, in fact, it makes sense to do it. Therefore, the impact therapist will offer his opinion or even suggest the client do something if he feels it would be helpful for the client. This often has quite an impact because the client has been wanting to do it but has been afraid, and now she feels that she has permission.

Example 1

Client:	He yells at me all the time. I hate it, but there isn't anything I can do. I just sit there and take it, crying usually.
Counselor:	Does he ever hit you?
Client:	No, he just complains and yells. I don't think he would hit me.
Counselor:	Do you think he would ever make you leave or threaten divorce?
Client:	No, he tells me he loves me and needs me all the time. His parents were both yellers, so I guess he got this from them.
Counselor:	Tanya, have you ever thought of saying something to him?
Client:	No, not really. I just thought as his wife I had to endure this.
Counselor:	No one should endure what you do. If you think you are not in any physical danger, it makes sense to me that you tell him how you feel when he yells.
Client:	You mean just tell him how I feel? Doesn't he know?
Counselor:	Probably not. You have every right not to be yelled at.
Client:	I do?
Counselor:	Yes. You do not have to be yelled at. There are better ways to talk to each other. I'm not sure what he'll do when you talk to him; but if you don't think he will hurt you, then from what you have told me, the worse thing he may do is yell, which is what he is doing now. Do you want to talk to him?
Client:	Yes.
Counselor:	Let's talk about when would be a good time to bring this up, and also let's practice what you might say to him.

In this example, the therapist saw that the client needed permission from someone to talk to her husband about her feelings. After checking out the safety of the situation, the therapist, in a sense, gave her permission. He also saw the need to discuss when and how to do this.

Example 2

Client: I beat up on myself all the time for not learning to play golf. I made a pledge to myself 3 years ago that I would learn how to play, but I haven't played more than four times since then. I keep my clubs out hoping that they'll get me to play. I just end up feeling bad.

Counselor: Have you ever considered that it's okay not to learn golf?

Client: No, I haven't. Are you saying that I could just put my clubs away for now and not beat up on myself?

Counselor: That's exactly what I'm saying.

Client: I've never considered giving up my demand to learn the game.

Counselor: You may someday decide to learn golf, but for now, I would say you need to give yourself permission to put your clubs away and do what you are currently doing.

Client: I feel like a heavy weight has just been lifted off my chest.

By the counselor simply telling the client it was okay not to learn golf, there was impact in that the client felt relieved; and she no longer had to beat up on herself.

Sometimes in a given session, I may use two, three, four, or even five of these paths, but I am definitely aware of what path I am using at any given time during a session. Many therapists do not think much about the path they are following—thus, they follow no path, and their sessions tend to wander and never focus. Those trained in Impact Therapy have found that, by following these paths, their sessions were clearer and more productive.

SUMMARY

There are a number of different ways to be impactful using Impact Therapy. Impact therapists help clients clarify their issues, help them increase awareness and understanding, and help them discover important things about themselves. Impact therapists also give support, provide encouragement, and give permission. Also, impact therapists help clients make decisions or help them stick with a decision once the decision has been made, and they help clients dispute their irrational or self-defeating beliefs. The impact therapist is always thinking about what the best way is to make the session helpful and impactful.

Chapter 4

Rapport

In this chapter, I present a fresh approach to rapport, the **R** of **RCFF**. The impact therapist views rapport building as an ongoing process that takes place during the contract, focus, and funnel phases, as well as during the initial phase of counseling. **Good rapport occurs when the client feels that the counselor is caring, competent, and most importantly, helpful.** Rapport building is very important and is something that the impact therapist is aware of throughout the entire counseling relationship and not just something that is done at the beginning of counseling. Students and workshop participants often ask me, "How long should I spend on gaining rapport?" I have two answers: "As much time as necessary; and this may be 2 minutes, 20 minutes, or 2 sessions," and "You are always working on rapport by being sensitive and helpful." **Being helpful is the best way to build rapport, and Impact Therapy emphasizes trying to be helpful.**

There has to be good rapport in order for there to be good counseling. If counselors have good rapport with their clients, the clients will tend to share more and be more open to different therapeutic interventions. Carl Rogers (1961) believed that the rapport or the relationship between a client and a therapist is often enough to move the client to better understanding or insight. He stated, "If I can provide a certain type of relationship, the other person will discover within himself the capacity to use that relationship for growth and change, and personal development will occur" (p. 33). While I do not fully agree with his position, I absolutely believe that rapport is an essential aspect of counseling. Without establishing and maintaining rapport, most sessions will go nowhere; and the therapist will have little impact. In this chapter, I talk about **initial rapport** and **ongoing rapport building**.

INITIAL RAPPORT BUILDING

All counselors are taught about rapport and the importance of building good rapport with the client. Most counselors use skills such as listening, clarification, reflection, and summarization during the opening few minutes of the first session. These skills are quite useful and necessary for certain clients but not for all clients. In this section,

I discuss the difference between nonproductive and productive initial rapport building. I start with nonproductive rapport building because, unfortunately, this is what many therapists do.

Nonproductive Initial Rapport Building

Counselors often spend far too much time in the initial session(s) building rapport when, in truth, there are many instances when rapport building is unnecessary. Some counselors just automatically devote the first half of the first session to rapport building and general information gathering when there does not need to be an initial rapport building phase. Instead, the counselor needs to listen briefly in order to grasp the issue and then go immediately into the contract or focus phase. In schools, mental health agencies, and hospitals, clients are often in a crisis and feel frustrated when the counselor uses the first 20 minutes of the session to build rapport when it is not needed. Many clients want to move to the heart of the matter as soon as possible. They do not want or need an extended rapport building phase.

I consider it nonproductive rapport building when the counselor wastes time with unnecessary clarifications, reflections, or irrelevant information gathering. It also is nonproductive to simply parrot back what the client just said, often starting with "What I hear you saying is…." Letting clients ramble the entire first session with the belief that it is necessary or helpful is also nonproductive rapport building. Below are examples of nonproductive initial rapport building. Later, I use the same examples and show productive rapport building.

Example 1

A client comes in wanting to talk about an issue regarding a coworker. This is the first time the therapist has met with the client.

Client: (*In a rapid, anxious-to-talk voice*) I am so glad you could see me. I have this situation at work, and it is driving me crazy. I work at the glass factory, and I know that one of my coworkers is stealing from the company. The company has told us that they are aware of stealing going on and if it does not stop, they may have to either close the plant or have an expensive investigation that would come out of all of our pockets. I don't know what to do.

Counselor: So you are having trouble at the glass plant due to a coworker. The coworker is stealing from the company, and the company is threatening to either close the plant or have an expensive investigation that would cost you some money. You are feeling confused about what to do.

Client:	That's right. I have a wife and three children, and I can't afford to lose my job or even lose some income. It is hard enough to make it as it is.
Counselor:	You have a wife and three kids, and you feel money is real tight for you.
Client:	Boy, money is tight. Just the other day I had to get $200 worth of work done on my car. It's old. I'll need a new one in a year or two. I just hope it will last that long. I have a son who will be going to college in a couple of years, and I just don't know where the money is going to come from. I wish my wife could work, but with two young children, I figure I come out ahead with her at home. Plus, she likes being at home when the kids are young. I like that, too.
Counselor:	You have an old car and a son who will be going to college in a year or two. Your wife stays home with the children, and you like that although you wish somehow there was more money. We'll just spend this first session getting to know each other. Tell me more about your family, your work at the factory, your worries about money, or any other aspect of your life that you would like to talk about.

In this example, the counselor believed that she must spend the first session in initial rapport building; thus, she used long, reflective responses as her main response. She allowed the topic to wander and even told the client that not much would happen during the first session. Although the client probably felt listened to, this was basically nonproductive rapport building and, therefore, not effective counseling.

Example 2

Client:	Can I talk to you, Mr. Gonzales?
Counselor:	Sure. You seem very upset.
Client:	I am in the 10th grade and go with Carol who is in the 11th grade. I heard from Fred that Carol wants to date Shawn, who is in the 12th grade. Shawn plays football, and I don't. I know that I don't have a chance with Carol.
Counselor:	(*Making sure that he is leaning slightly toward the client, with his hands folded*) Bill, what I hear you saying is that you are in the 10th grade, and your girlfriend is in the 11th grade, and you think she wants to date a 12th grader who plays football. You also are saying that you don't feel like you now have a chance to keep Carol as your girlfriend.

Client: Yeah, Carol and I have been dating for 3 months, and we have gotten along pretty well until last week. We had a fight because I think she flirts too much with other guys, so I said something to her. She said she didn't flirt and didn't like me telling her what she can and cannot do.

Counselor: What I hear you saying is that you and Carol have been dating for 3 months, and you had a fight last week over your believing that she flirts too much. You also said she told you that she didn't think she flirted, and she didn't like you telling her want she can and cannot do.

In this nonproductive scenario, the counselor restricted himself to reflection only, wasting valuable time and possibly turning Bill off since he was in a crisis. The counselor believed he was building rapport.

Productive Initial Rapport Building

The impact therapist always assesses the amount of time that seems to be needed for initial rapport building. Initial rapport building has to do with whether or not the client feels comfortable with the counselor and feels ready to talk. There are times when the client is very eager to talk, so initial rapport building is minimal. There are other times when the counselor has to take much time to gain the trust of the client. **The impact therapist will spend only as much time as needed in initial rapport building**, using traditional rapport building responses and also responses like the ones listed below.

These responses can be used in the initial moments of counseling or any time they seem appropriate. The responses show the counselor is listening, cares, and is trying to move the session along. All these responses are given with an understanding voice and facial expression that shows care and concern.

- Say some more. (*A brief response instead of a long paraphrase*)
- I think I can help you. Obviously, you are in some pain. I'd like to hear a little more, and then I'll see what I can do to be helpful.
- I am not sure where you are going with this, and I need to know in order to know what to be listening for. Can you tell me where you are heading with your story?
- I don't need all the details, and it doesn't seem to me that telling the details is that helpful to you. The more time we have for working on the problem, the better.
- I am going to ask you to cut the story short so we can focus on what would be helpful to you. I'm afraid that if you tell the entire story, we won't have any time to do the healing work that is needed.

- Would it be helpful to take a few minutes to work on this issue? It seems to me that would be a good use of our time.
- I think I would rather focus in on one issue rather than just touch on a whole bunch of issues. I'm wondering, could it be that your wanting to tell me all the issues is your way of avoiding going deeper?
- Let's back up to something you said earlier. I am still thinking about....
- I want to make sure that we accomplish something during this session. What would be helpful?
- As I hear you, there are four different issues that you want to deal with. Let's list them and then decide the best way to spend our time. It is important that we not waste time since there is much to cover.

I offer these examples as different from the standard, reflective responses. (Certainly, there are many times when reflection and clarification are excellent responses.) Impact therapists build rapport by moving the session along and trying to make the session meaningful.

The following two examples were presented above but have now been altered to illustrate productive rapport.

Example 1

A client comes in wanting to talk about an issue regarding a coworker. This is the first time the therapist has met with the client.

Client: (*In a rapid, anxious-to-talk voice*) I am so glad you could see me. I have this situation at work, and it is driving me crazy. I work at the glass factory, and I know that one of my coworkers is stealing from the company. The company has told us that they are aware of stealing going on and if it does not stop, they may have to either close the plant or have an expensive investigation that would come out of all of our pockets. I don't know what to do.

Counselor: I am not sure what you mean when you say you don't know what to do?

Client: The coworker is a friend of mine. I would hate to get him in trouble, but he's jeopardizing my job and my family.

Counselor: Sounds like a tough situation. I think by the time we finish today, you'll have a better idea of what to do. Let me ask you a question? How much time do you think you have before the company will act on the stealing problem?

Client: They said by the end of the month, so only a couple of weeks.

Counselor: That's good. So you'll have some time to reflect on what we talk about, and then we can get together again. How does that sound?

Client: Good! I am glad to have someone to talk to. This has been on my mind for days—ever since the meeting they had with us.

Counselor: I'm sure it has. I guess we need to look at the choices you have and the pros and cons of each of the choices. Does that seem like a good place to start?

Client: Yeah. Whatever you think.

In this example, the impact therapist saw that there was no need for extended, initial rapport building. She moved almost immediately to the contract phase and then to the focus phase. She believed the client would feel she was with him since her focus was on the issue that was pressing, namely his work situation. Rapport was being built by her ability to rather quickly focus the session and make it helpful.

Example 2

Client: Can I talk to you, Mr. Gonzales?

Counselor: Sure. You seem very upset.

Client: I am in the 10th grade and go with Carol who is in the 11th grade. I heard from Fred that Carol wants to date Shawn, who is in the 12th grade. Shawn plays football, and I don't. I know that I don't have a chance with Carol.

Counselor: (*With a concerned voice*) Why do you say you don't have a chance?

Client: We had a fight last week because I accused her of flirting, and Shawn's a 12th grader! (In a very excited, hurried voice) I don't know what I am going to do!

Counselor: (*In a calm, concerned voice*) I think I can help you take a look at the relationship, and together we can talk about some possible strategies. First, it may be good to look at what the facts are and decide if you may be making more of this than you need to. (*Going to his large wipe board, begins to write on the board*) Bill, let's look at what you know, such as you had a fight last week, and what you are imagining.

Client: I know I am going to lose her! I, uh,…

Counselor: Wait a minute, how do you know that? You might be right, but let's slow down. I want you to talk about the good parts of the relationship and why Carol wanted to date you to begin with.

The counselor used many different responses and moved the session along rather quickly since he saw that Bill was upset. The therapist felt rapport could be built during the contract and focus phase, rather than engaging in any extended initial rapport building. The therapist went to the wipe board and started writing because he felt this would help Bill to focus. He did not let Bill ramble. The counselor's actions and words communicated that help was on its way.

ONGOING RAPPORT

The impact therapist views rapport building as an ongoing process. The therapist pays careful attention to the relationship since he understands that he is moving at a rather rapid rate. If ever it appears that the client is uncomfortable with the pace or focus, the impact therapist will either slow down, change the focus, or ask the client for some feedback. The impact therapist tries not to move too quickly but does try to move the session below **7** so that there is new insight or awareness. Sessions below **7** usually lead to rapport building because the counselor is seen as being helpful.

The confidence of the therapist plays a part in rapport building. Ideally, the impact therapist will present herself with confidence since this helps the client to believe in the counselor and the counseling process. One other way that the impact therapist builds rapport throughout all the RCFF phases is to engage the Adult ego state of the client as much as possible. That is, the impact therapist gets the client to think and respond from the Adult whenever possible. This tends to contribute to positive rapport because the client feels respected by the counselor.

Impact therapists feel free to have a wide range of responses, including reflection, clarification, questioning, summarizing, probing, and teaching. In the examples below, the counselor uses his voice, eyes, comments, and knowledge to build rapport.

Example 1

Client: I don't know why I am here. No one can help me. I did a terrible thing. I am so ashamed.

Counselor: (*Using a slow, calm voice and facial gestures that indicate concern*) Obviously, something is bothering you. You feel you did a terrible thing. I hope you can talk about it since you feel so badly about whatever it is that you did.

Client: I don't think I can tell you. I don't want anyone to know.

Counselor: (*Leaning forward, looking at the client with concern and compassion, using a soft, calm voice*) It's okay if you tell me, and it is okay if you don't. I see your pain, and that is what I want to help you with. No matter what you did, my job as the counselor is to try to help you get some perspective on whatever it was and to not have so much pain. Let's talk about either why you are afraid to tell, or you can just tell me what happened. (*Pause*) Or we can talk about you for a few minutes.

Example 2

Client: (*In a depressed, manipulating voice*) You are my last hope. I've seen two other counselors, and they gave up on me. They said I wasn't motivated. I don't know if I can go on. I hate my life. All I do is go to work and then watch television at night. Weekends are hard because they are so long. My life has been hell, and I don't see any way that it can get better. If counselors can't help me, then how am I suppose to figure it out?

Counselor: (*Deciding to use a matter-of-fact voice instead of matching the client's depressed voice since it seemed somewhat manipulative*) Tell me what the other counselors tried that did not work so that I won't try them, too.

Client: (*Still looking down, talking in a depressed manner*) Uh, well, let me think. They tried to get me to meet people, do different things, but I told them I was too afraid.

Counselor: (*Using an energetic voice*) Let me get this straight. (*Pulling up a chair across from the client*) You are wanting to move from your "I hate my life" chair to a "better life" chair.

Client: (*Looks up at the other chair and then to the counselor; talks in a rather puzzled, interested voice*) Yeah, but I don't know how to do it.

Counselor: (*Using a calm voice with a very relaxed pace; looking more at the chair than at the client*) Then our goal is to get you to move from where you are to over here. Now in order to do that, I would think you are going to have to change some things. Can you get to this seat any other way than getting up and moving?

Client: (*Thinks for a minute*) No, I guess not.

Counselor: Well, then our contract is to get you to move, and I realize that there is a part of you that is going to fight doing that because you are familiar with being in your depressed seat.

Client: How did you know that?

Counselor: (*Confidently*) It is my job to be able to understand how people feel. I am willing to help if you'll do your part. And you know what, your part is bigger than mine, but I've learned a lot of ways to help people like you.

These two examples give some idea how the impact therapist goes about building rapport. The skillful use of his voice, body, and facial expressions contributed greatly to rapport because they showed the client that he cared. The therapist, instead of just listening, tried to make something happen in each of these sessions.

RAPPORT WITH DIFFICULT CLIENTS

Much attention has to be given to rapport building when the client is forced (by the law, parents, or an agency) to talk to a therapist. There are definitely some techniques therapists can use that may help. Sometimes, a warm, kind, caring voice helps build rapport with difficult clients. Often, traditional rapport building behaviors (looking at the client, leaning toward the client, reflections) that work with most clients may be detrimental when trying to build rapport with the resistant client. There may be times when the counselor may want to look away as the client is talking, especially with teenagers. Slouching, watering plants, or checking fingernails may be better for rapport building than looking directly at the client.

With nonvolunteer clients, the impact therapist will try to hook the client by making the counseling interesting which, in turn, helps build rapport. ("Hook" the client means getting him to interact with the counselor and eventually engage in the counseling process.) The therapist may ask questions that do not pertain at all to the purpose of the session—asking about interests, sports, movies, cars, work, or general background, purposely letting the client ramble about seemingly irrelevant matters. However, this strategy is not a good idea for clients who are ready to talk. The counselor also may decide to talk about different subjects or even tell interesting stories that are somewhat related to the client's problem. The purpose of this is twofold—the client might relate to what is said, and an uncomfortable, nonproductive silence is prevented. (With nonvolunteer clients, long silences usually are not helpful.)

I often use some creative techniques, such as drawings, movement, chairs, or props, early in the first session with resistant clients in hopes of getting them interested or curious. With young children who do not want to talk, I use puppets, games, or play therapy in order to gain rapport. I especially try many different things when it is apparent that traditional counseling simply will not work. My guiding principle when I think I am going to lose the client if I don't do something different is "try things; it can't hurt." Too often, beginning counselors play it safe. They do what they were taught, and the client does not return because no rapport was established. These counselors will then tend to blame the client's not returning on the client and never even consider that their own "traditional" counseling responses may have contributed to the client's not returning. By traditional, I mean reflecting, showing concern, and looking at the client.

Impact therapists will use nontraditional responses such as looking away, talking about seemingly irrelevant topics, or using an almost disinterested voice when appropriate.

Nonproductive Rapport Building With Traditional Responses

Example

Counselor: How can I be of help?

Client: (*Angrily*) You can't. Get the damn protective service people off my back. That's what you can do. You're just out to make money off me too! How many times do I have to be here until I get my kids back?!

Counselor: You want to know how long you are to come here, and you are feeling angry right now.

Client: You're damn right I am. Wouldn't you be angry if someone took your kids away because you whipped them. Nobody is going to tell me what I can do with my kids, and you better not try!

Counselor: You're saying that you believe your kids were taken away from you because you whipped them. You are worried that I am going to tell you what to do with your kids. I can see that you are very upset.

Client:	No shit. If you keep talking to me this way, I am going to be even angrier!!

The counselor's comments consisted of reflecting back what the client said. This was not good for rapport because the client was very angry about having to be in counseling. The client did not perceive the counselor to be sincere.

Productive Rapport Building With Nontraditional Responses

Example 1

Counselor:	How can I be of help?
Client:	You can't. Get the damn protective service people off my back. That's what you can do. You're just out to make money off me too! How many times do I have to be here until I get my kids back?!
Counselor:	(*Speaking slowly with no intensity—very casual, looking away and then back at the client, sort of like Columbo, if you know that character from television*) You know, I'm not sure how many times you have to come. I know it is a pain to be here. I do want to try to help. In fact, I can understand that you might not trust me right now. I wish you could believe that I am on your side in that I would like to be of help to you. (*Voice pattern is key.*)
Client:	Yeah, right. You're not on my side. All of you are out to get me!
Counselor:	(*Calmly*) I went to school to learn to help people, not to "get" them. I always know there are two sides to any story, and I am curious about your side of the story. The story I heard had to do with this (*pulls out a 3 foot high, plastic beer bottle*).
Client:	(*Blinks his eyes, then stares at the bottle; using an inquisitive voice*) What did you hear about my drinking?
Counselor:	I heard….

In this example, the counselor used her voice and manner in the session to try to put the client at ease. She also worded her comments in such a way as to get the client curious, and then she used the beer bottle, all in hopes the client would get comfortable enough to be willing to talk.

Example 2

Counselor: Hi, Art, how can I be of help?

Client: I am not going to talk to you. My parents may be able to make me come, but I don't have to talk. You can't make me!

Counselor: (*Seeing that the teenager is not at all interested in being at the session, the counselor looks away and slouches in his chair, rather than make direct eye contact.*) You know, you're right. I hate it when parents do this to me, that is, make their kids come. I usually can work pretty well with kids who want to be here; but when they're here under pressure, it's tough. Sounds like a relationship where parents are up here (*pulls up a child's chair; counselor stands in her chair; client looks up with a puzzled look*), and they want you to be here (*points at the child's chair; client looks at it*). This parents up here and kids down there causes all kinds of problems. I always hate it when kids think they are sick or something because they are here. Sure, there are problems, but it usually is a combination of things. (*Counselor sits back down*.)

Client: I hate it when my parents treat me like a little kid! They want me to be just like my goody-two-shoes sisters. Well, I'm not, but I'm not sick. So I don't like school, I'm still passing everything, but they want all A's. I skipped school the other day, and they act like I robbed a bank or something.

Again, the counselor used a very relaxed body posture and specially worded phrases to try to get the teenager's attention. She also stood on the chair and used the small chair to make things more dramatic and more concrete. By using these rather nontraditional methods of rapport building, the client loosened up and began to talk.

Example 3

Client: I am not talking to you. It's that stupid teacher. She's an idiot. She deserved what she got. All I did was curse a little.

Counselor: It is obvious you're upset.

Client: (*Folds arms*) I said I am not talking to you!

Counselor: I'd like to hear your version of what happened.

Client: I said I wasn't talking to you (*turns away*).

Counselor: That's fine. I guess I'll just have to make up what happened. You sure you don't want to talk?

Client: Yeah, I'm sure. I'm not talking!

Counselor: I guess the only thing I can do is have a drawing. (*Tears a sheet of paper into three sections; client watches with a questioning look; counselor writes something on each of the sheets and then folds the sheets.*) Do you want to draw, or do you want me to?

Client: What's on the sheets?

Counselor: Three different possibilities as to what happened.

Client: Do you want to know what happened? I'll tell you what happened.

Counselor: (*Nods and listens as the client tells her story*) That was helpful to hear your version. I think I can be of help to you and the teacher. Seems to me that both of you played a part in this. Which do you want to talk about first, her role or yours?

In each of the nontraditional, productive rapport building examples above, the therapist did something a little out of the ordinary since she felt that the traditional rapport building techniques of reflection were not going to work.

SOME QUESTIONS TO ASK YOURSELF ABOUT RAPPORT BUILDING

For some therapists, rapport building is very easy, while, for others, it is something that must be given much attention throughout the therapy process. The best way to determine if rapport building is easy for you is to ask yourself some of these questions: How easily do people talk to me? How easily do people trust me? Are people generally comfortable with me? Honest input from family, friends, and fellow students or coworkers may help in determining how much you need to work on your rapport building techniques. Following are some good questions to ask in reference to a specific counseling session:

- Do I feel comfortable in the session?
- Do my nonverbal cues as well as my verbal cues let the client know I am truly interested and want to help?
- Does the client seem comfortable?
- Am I focused on helping the client, or am I worried about how I am doing as a counselor?

CONTINUING SESSION EXAMPLE

I conclude this chapter and the next three chapters with an ongoing case example of Impact Therapy in order to give you a sense of what happens during a session using the **RCFF** map. The case example deals with Don who came to me for counseling due to anxiety. In the opening segment, I focus on rapport building. The rapport building phase is rather short because Don was eager to talk and had a good idea as to what was bothering him.

Ed:	Hi, I'm Ed. Have a seat over here.
Client:	Hi. I'm Don.
Ed:	Nice to meet you. How can I be of help?
Don:	I've been anxious lately, sort of like anxiety attacks. I wake up often and seem nervous, and throughout the day, I often don't feel right. I can't concentrate very well on anything. It is hard to study. I feel like it's taking me twice as long to get my assignments done.

Ed: *(With a soft, concerned voice)* I am sure that doesn't feel very good. Do you have any idea as to what might be causing this?

Don: I don't know. I'm in school at the University. I'm a sophomore. My girlfriend, Jan, is at another university. She's a freshman. I think that is part of it. I just seem to be nervous all the time.

Ed: Love relationships often can be a source of anxiety. School can also be a source of stress. Tell me more about this nervousness.

Don: I just feel nervous. I worry about how I am going to do on tests, what I am going to do when I graduate, what my girlfriend is doing, and if she is going to cheat on me. We just got back together this summer. We were broken up for 6 months because she did cheat on me, but now she says she loves me.

Ed: You have been back together for close to 7 months. Have you worried about her cheating on you all this time?

Don: No. Not the first semester. Things were great. We'd see each other every other weekend at least. We had a great time going to the football games, and then Christmas was good. We went to Colorado on a skiing trip. This semester has been different. I can't concentrate. I can't believe there are only 6 more weeks left in the semester. This whole semester has been a blur. I've got to decide about summer school?

Ed: Did anything happen to trigger this change?

Don: Well, yes. I got a call the second week of the semester from one of my friends who goes to school where she does, and he said he saw her out for lunch with this guy. I asked her about it, and she said it was nothing, just a guy she studies with.

Ed: *(I felt that I was gaining valuable information from the answers to the questions.)* Do you believe her?

Don: I don't know. I want to. She cheated on me once already, and that's when we broke up. She and I were friends before we started dating. She was dating Tony, and I know she cheated on him three different times. I think about that all the time. I've lost interest in almost everything. I don't go out with friends. I stopped body building. Body building used to be what I lived for.

Ed:	*(With a soft, caring voice)* If you enjoy body building, why did you quit doing that?
Don:	I don't know. I just stopped caring sort of. If she doesn't care about me, then what's the use of doing anything. Body building was my life besides her. In high school I was somebody because I was big, and everyone knew of me. I've lost 30 pounds in the last 4 months. I can't seem to be interested in anything.
Ed:	*(Because school can be the source of much anxiety, I wanted to find out if it was a problem.)* How is school going for you?
Don:	I'm doing okay. I feel some pressure since I dropped down to 12 hours. All I do is study and think about her. Like last night when I called her, she was tired; so I have been worried ever since, wondering if she is going to break up with me. She just didn't seem excited to talk.
Ed:	From what you are telling me, it sounds like she's on the verge of breaking up. Has she indicated this to you at all?
Don:	No, quite the contrary. She says she loves me and hopes we get married. She does tell me she does not like my insecurity.
Ed:	What about friends here? Do you go out with them at all, say, to eat or to the movies or to study?
Don:	I did last semester more than now. Come to think of it, I have not gone out hardly at all this semester. Being so nervous seems to take so much out of me.
Ed:	Have you ever felt like this before in your life?
Don:	Sort of. When I went from 5th to 6th grade and changed schools. I was a nervous wreck for a long time. I don't like the unknown or new things very much. I like to know how things are going to be.
Ed:	*(In trying to understand the client better, I sought some family history.)* Do either of your parents worry a lot?
Don:	They both do. Dad especially. He worries about everything. He's an unhappy man. He worries a lot about Mom. They were separated once when I was 13, but he begged her to come back even though he knew she had been with this other man. She actually took off to Florida for 3 months with the guy.
Ed:	What was that like for you?

Don:	I was with my dad, and it was tough. He'd cry, and I would try to comfort him. We tried all kinds of things to find her.
Ed:	That's helpful information. Let's come back to you and try to figure out how these sessions can be beneficial. Don, what were you hoping to get from counseling?
Don:	I don't know. I just want to feel better.
Ed:	Would you say that much of this centers around your girlfriend?
Don:	Yes, I guess so. I had not quite seen it that way, but as I tell you what's going on, it does seem to point to her. She's great though.
Ed:	Except for your not feeling like you can trust her.
Don:	But is that just in my head? She says I can trust her.
Ed:	(*In a soft, kind voice*) I think we need to take a look at your relationship. Your love seems almost like an addiction. There is a book on that subject that I'd like you to read.
Don:	It does feel like an addiction. I'm willing to do anything that can help.
Ed:	Also, we need to look at how you feel about yourself and where good feelings about yourself come from.
Don:	I've always worried about what others thought of me. I just don't know what would help me.
Ed:	I have some ideas.

At this point I felt there was good rapport, and I had a fairly good idea as to what was going on with Don. I gathered some useful data about Don regarding body building and school. Also, the information regarding the family history was helpful to understand Don's world in that he has parents who worry, especially his father regarding his relationship with Don's mother. Plus, he saw his mom cheat on his dad. I chose not to go into any great detail regarding the family history since I felt the session could be more productive by dealing with Don's pressing problem. Although much more information could have been gathered, I felt more time spent on initial rapport building was not necessary and would probably be nonproductive, so I moved to the next phase, the contract phase. I figured that I would get additional information as the need arose.

SUMMARY

Rapport building is an essential part of Impact Therapy (the **R** in **RCFF**). Impact therapists believe that being helpful is the best way to build rapport, and thus, it is an ongoing process. Getting the client to think from his Adult ego state shows respect for client and empowers the client and, thus, builds rapport. Rapport is seen as something to monitor not only in the beginning of counseling but also throughout each phase of counseling. Impact therapists are aware that sometimes initial rapport is almost instant, so they move quickly to the contract, focus, and funnel phases while paying attention to ongoing rapport building. Impact therapists emphasize productive rapport building whereas other counselors often engage in nonproductive rapport building. The impact therapist is also willing to use nontraditional responses when rapport building is difficult.

Chapter 5

Contract

In the Introduction, I discussed **RCFF** as the heart of Impact Therapy. The **C** stands for **Contract**. The impact therapist believes that within each session there should be a contract which helps both the counselor and the client stay focused. By contract, I mean an understanding as to what the client wants or needs to work on, discuss, explore, or decide. Too often, counselors work without a contract, which tends to lead to a session that goes from topic to topic.

ESTABLISHING A CONTRACT

Establishing a contract is essential to the counseling process. The contract organizes the session. Also, rapport can be built during the contract phase, especially when the client feels that the therapist is tuned in to his problems and is trying to be understanding regarding what it is that he wants to resolve. Impact Therapy is an approach to counseling where the therapist has a clear understanding as to the direction of the therapy—the contract provides that direction. When clients come for counseling, they sometimes know exactly why they have come; then again, there are times when clients are very unclear as to why they have come—they just know something is wrong. When the client is unclear, the impact therapist will use an extended contract phase in order to clarify the goal and purpose of the session and perhaps of subsequent sessions. In Impact Therapy terms, the contract needs to be established so that the counselor knows what issues or points to **focus** and **funnel**.

Many times, obtaining the contract will include getting "permission" to discuss an issue more in-depth. There may be one, two, or more contracts during a single session. When an issue gets finished, resolved, or understood, another contract for additional work needs to emerge or be made. It is also important to understand that the contract may change during the session as the counselor sees new and more important issues to focus on. During a session, an impact therapist is always aware of the contract and constantly monitors whether or not the contract needs to be changed or revised. The following examples illustrate the contract phase of counseling. Reference to the client and counselor's voices is continually made to emphasize that awareness of voice is essential to the impact therapist.

Example 1

Counselor: I would like to see you work through this issue with your dad. It seems to me that there is a lot of unresolved pain.

Client: (*Beginning to cry*) Oh, there is. The stuff about my mom is hard enough. I don't know about taking on the dad issue.

Counselor: (*In a nurturing, yet strong voice*) I don't think you can resolve your relationship problems unless you get finished with your dad. I'd like to see you do that now. I know your Child is scared, but your Adult does want to get on with her life.

Client: Just thinking about working on it is scary.

Counselor: I know, but it is worth it, and I know you can handle whatever comes up. You seem ready.

Client: Okay. I think you are right. I am ready to finish this business with my dad. How do I start?

Counselor: Why don't we start by putting your dad in the empty chair (*from Gestalt therapy—client had done some empty chair work in previous sessions*). What would you want to say to him?

Establishing a contract is often very easy as in the example above. Most of the time, the contract is a mutually agreed upon decision by the counselor and the client. However, there are times when the experienced counselor understands what is needed and then proceeds since the contract is implied rather than stated.

Example 2

Counselor: How can I help?

Client: (*In a very hurried, eager voice*) I am so glad that you could see me. My neighbor, Joan, told me that you were easy to talk to. I am married and have been for 21 years. I was married before when I was 18, but I never told my current husband about this. I was only married for 4 years. Anyway, what has happened is I got a call from some lawyer in California, and he said that I was left $10,000 by my ex-husband. I haven't even been in contact with him for over 20 years. I don't know what to do. Do I tell my husband? Do I refuse the money, which I do need? Do I take the money but not tell my husband? Boy, this is a mess!!

Counselor: (*Purposely using a calm voice*) First of all, this is what I call a pleasant problem. The worse that can happen is you are financially exactly where you were before you received this phone call. Let's talk about each of the options you laid out, and I think that by the end of the session you'll have a lot better idea what you want to do.

In this example, the counselor realized that he did not have to spend time on rapport or the contract since there was an implied contract. He could immediately start trying to help the client explore her options.

If the contract is not implied, one of the simplest ways to get a contract is to ask the client what it is that she wants to work on.

Example 3

Counselor: I am not sure which part of all this you want to work on. Do you want to talk about how to be a better parent or how to stop all the fighting that goes on in your house, especially between you and your husband?

Client: I think both are important.

Counselor: I do too, but I think counseling will go better if we deal with them separately since they are different issues. Which one would you like to start with?

Client: I think my husband.

Counselor: Okay. Am I right in assuming that you would like to quit fighting?

Client: I think I do.

Counselor: What do you mean by "I think I do"?

Client: We're so used to fighting. I don't know if we'd know how to act if we didn't fight.

Counselor: Let's look at the fighting, the purpose it serves, and ways to interact instead of fighting. Would that be a good way to spend the next 40 minutes?

Client: Yes, I want to quit fighting.

Example 4

Counselor: You've mentioned a number of things that are bothering you. Which one do you want to work on?

Client: I don't know.

Counselor: I think it is real important that we pick one issue and stay with that one until you feel like you have a handle on it. Otherwise, I'm afraid we'll be all over the place, dealing some with riding the school bus, some with your mom, some with your stepdad, and some with your dad. Which one do you want to work on first?

Client: My dad or riding the school bus.

Counselor: Let's do the school bus since it is something you do 5 days a week.

Client: I don't know what you can do to help me. Those kids are mean.

Counselor: I'm pretty sure that we can figure something out that will help you. I want to make sure we stay on this one topic for a while. Now when you start to talk about some of the other things that bother you, I'm going to remind you of our contract which is to focus on how to make riding the school bus a better experience for you.

In the above examples, the therapist worked to get a clear contract with the client. The therapist certainly indicated to the client that there needed to be a contract to work on one issue. Too often, therapists never make this clear to the client. My intent is not to imply that a counselor has to rigidly stick to a single issue, but rather I want to point out that a contract can be very helpful in focusing both the counselor and the client. Far too often when there is no contract, the counseling goes from topic to topic, going *10, 9, 8, – 10, 9, 8, – 10, 9, 8* — never going below *7*.

In the next examples, the therapist had a contract to work on one issue but then switched the contract because of what was emerging. This often occurs. The therapist needs to remember to always be aware of the contract because it determines what to focus and funnel.

Example 5

Counselor: So you want us to work on helping you to not fight with your husband.

Client: That would be great. We've only been married for 6 months; and if it is this bad now, who knows what it'll be like 10 years from now. I don't know how to keep him from getting upset because he is mad that I slept with this guy before I met him. There's nothing I can do about that.

Counselor: How often does this subject come up?

Client: Lots of times. At least two or three times a week.

Counselor: How does this subject come up? What are the circumstances when he brings this up?

Client: It can be almost any evening or time when we have been out at a bar or for dinner.

Counselor: Has he been drinking?

Client: Probably.

Counselor: Have you ever had this fight when he has not been drinking?

Client: Well, (*pause*) come to think of it, it has been after he's been drinking.

Counselor: Is drinking a big part of his life?

Client: Oh yes, and I drink very rarely.

Counselor: (*Seeing the need to change the contract to conducting an alcohol assessment*) I want to ask you a number of questions about your husband's drinking. Do you think your husband has a drinking problem?

Client: Not like my dad has. He is terrible. He drinks all the time. He hasn't worked for the last 10 years because of his drinking. I am so glad I met my husband because if not, I'd probably still be living there.

Counselor: We'll probably come back to your dad in a minute, but let me ask you some more about your husband's drinking. Do you know if your husband's parents have or had a drinking problem?

The counselor saw that more than likely the problem had to do with the client's husband's drinking, so she shifted the contract to conducting an alcohol assessment. The reason for this is if there is an alcohol problem, that problem has to be addressed first before any others can be since alcohol in the family creates so many problems. My experience has taught me that having extensive knowledge about addictions counseling is absolutely necessary to be an effective counselor. So many problems seen in schools, colleges, mental health centers, and other treatment facilities stem from addiction in the client's history.

Example 6

Counselor: Hi. I'm Mr. Jacobs. What is your name?

Client: I'm Marvin.

Counselor: What did you want to talk about?

Client:	I need to get along better in school. I get in trouble all the time. That's why I'm here now.
Counselor:	I think I can help. What grade are you in?
Client:	Third.
Counselor:	(*Establishing the contract*) You want me to help you to get along better here at school?
Client:	Yes. No one wants to be my friend.
Counselor:	Do you have any ideas why they don't want to be friends?
Client:	The teacher says I'm bossy, and I don't know how to cooperate.
Counselor:	Do you think that's true?
Client:	No one ever helps me out. Why should I help them out? I've got to be tough.
Counselor:	(*Wanting to understand the client's private logic*) I don't understand what you mean when you say you have to be tough.
Client:	You would if you came from my home. I hate this new guy Mom is living with. I liked where we used to live. I didn't want to move here. My dad is back home, a thousand miles away!! And this new dude is mean. Mom makes me call him Dad. I hate calling him that. He's not my dad!
Counselor:	(*Believing that his home life is affecting his school life, wants to establish a new contract*) Have you had a chance to talk to anyone about moving here and how your life has changed?
Client:	No.
Counselor:	It sure seems to me that you have gone through quite a bit. Talking may help. I think you have all kinds of feelings inside.
Client:	(*Tears up*) I miss my dad....

The counselor went quickly to the contract phase rather than spending time with rapport. The counselor also changed the contract when he saw that talking about Dad was more important than talking about school. Too, it is important to note that this session was less than 2 minutes old, and the counselor was focusing on something very significant. By moving quickly, the counselor may have had time to talk about the dad and then tie these feelings into how the child was acting in school.

There are times when establishing the contract is more difficult. The client may ramble, be confused, or have a number of issues and not be able to decide which one to focus on first. Below are a number of examples of when the contract phase would be difficult and lengthy.

Getting a Contract When the Client Is Rambling

Example

Counselor: We've been talking for at least 10 minutes, and I am not sure what it is that you want help with.

Client: I don't know. I am not sure if I want to play basketball or try out for cheerleader. I know that I want to do something that gets me in front of the boys. That's terrible. I wish I didn't feel like I always had to have a boyfriend. Heck, my mom goes through boyfriends all the time. I don't like the guy she is with now. He's not nice to me, and I don't like the way he looks at me either. He's creepy.

Counselor: (*Using a calm, deliberate voice*) Susie, I'm trying to figure out what is most pressing for you. Do you want to figure out the basketball/cheerleader thing?

Client: My mom says I should do cheerleading. She was a cheerleader, and she thinks I'll get more dates that way. I think Vince is interested in me. He's cute, but he's shorter than me. What do you think about dating someone shorter than me?

Counselor: Wait a second. We don't have any agreement as to what we are talking about. You keep changing subjects. I want you to slow down and think about what you want to talk about.

Client: I do this all the time. I think about so many things at once.

Counselor: I see that. I think my task as the counselor is to get you to focus on one issue at a time. You'll be surprised at how much you can learn about yourself if we focus on only one thing. And before we're finished with counseling, we probably will want to look at your habit of thinking about so many things at once.

The counselor in this example became very aware of the client's tendency to ramble. She knew she had to keep working on getting a contract with the girl or the session would never go below **7**.

Getting a Contract When the Client Is Confused

Example

Client: I don't know if I should try to go back to my old job or not. The doctors say that it will be too demanding on me physically, but I sort of think I might be able to do it. I feel fine right now. But I don't want to hurt myself either, and the doctors say that could happen if I start lifting things and moving things. My supervisor told me that he wants me back. My wife said she absolutely does not want me to go back to that job because of what the doctors said. I think it probably would be best that I look at other jobs, but working at the warehouse is all that I know. I like working there. I don't even know how to go about looking for another job.

Counselor: You have a lot going on. I would imagine it is confusing.

Client: I am real confused. Sometimes I think of working at my old job. Sometimes I think of working at the warehouse but in some new position, and sometimes I think of trying to find another job. I just go round and round inside my head.

Counselor: I think you're confused because you are thinking about so many things at once. As you have been talking, I have been sorting some of this out in my head. Here's what I hear. The first thing you need to decide is whether you can go back to your old job since that would be your first choice. Once that is decided and if you decide you should not go back, then we should probably take a look at the various options which include possibly working at the warehouse doing something else or finding a job elsewhere.

Client: But how do I know if I can go back or not unless I go try it?

Counselor: Let's spend a few minutes trying to figure out whether you should go back to your old job. Can we agree to do that?

Client: Okay, but I don't know how to determine if I should go back.

Counselor: I have some ideas, but I need us first to agree to stay on that subject. Let me write this out for you, and we can talk from this chart.

WANT TO GO BACK	ABLE TO GO BACK
Yes	*?*
	Doctor's comments
	How you feel physically
	Wife's opinion

In the above example, the counselor helped clarify what the client was saying and then made sure she had a contract about deciding if the man was able to go back to his old job. She used the chart to focus the client on the contract.

Getting a Contract When the Client Has a Number of Issues

Example

Client: I don't think Missy likes me. She plays with Joan now instead of me.

Counselor: Would you like to talk about that some more?

Client: I don't know. I had a fight with my mom last night about having to go visit my dad this weekend. I don't want to go. It's no fun. He often leaves me there with his new wife, and I don't like her. Well, really, I don't think she likes me or my mom.

Counselor: That sounds like something we could talk about.

Client: See, my mom and dad still fight on the phone a lot. Mom wants Dad to pay the money he's suppose to pay. Delores, my dad's wife, thinks my mom shouldn't ask for the money. Mom even makes me ask Dad for the money (*starts to cry*).

Counselor: (*Using a nurturing voice*) I bet it doesn't feel good to be in the middle of the fighting.

Client: No, it doesn't. That's why I like school. But if Missy doesn't want to be my friend, then school even makes me sad.

Counselor: Caroline, you've mentioned a number of things that are bothering you. I'm not sure which of these we should talk about first.

Client:　　　There are other things that I could tell you about.

Counselor:　If they are real important, I want to hear them. Right now, I am just trying to figure out from what you have told me so far what would be the best thing to talk about. I'd like us to decide on one thing to talk about for the remainder of the time that we have today.

Client:　　　Which one do you think?

Counselor:　That's a tough question. Let's list them here on the board so that you can see all the things you want to talk about. All of them seem important—you and Missy, this weekend, your feeling in the middle of your mom and dad, and your relationship with your dad's new wife. Maybe we can do two topics today if we have time.

Caroline's List of Things to Work On

Missy
This weekend
Being in the Middle of Mom and Dad
Dad's new Wife

Client:　　　I think I want to talk about Missy and why she doesn't like me. And then can we talk about being in the middle.

Counselor:　Okay. Let's take a look at your relationship with Missy. Tell me more about what is going on.

In this example, all the issues seemed important, but the counselor went with the one that the client chose. Seeing the list helped the client to prioritize her concerns. Often the impact therapist will use visual techniques such as lists, props, or chairs during the contract phase because they help to clarify the problem.

Getting a Contract When the Client Is Forced To Be in Therapy

It is important to realize that there almost always will be contract difficulties when the client is forced by a judge, principal, agency, spouse, or parents to be in therapy. When the client is forced to be in counseling or does not want to be at the session, the contract phase usually becomes a long, drawn out process. In one sense, the contract, or the goal, is implied—that is, to get the client to be willing to talk.

Too often, the novice counselor goes ahead with trying to get the client to talk about the issues that brought him into counseling before there is rapport and before there is any willingness on the part of the client to work on anything. The impact therapist realizes that any contract for productive work with a nonvoluntary client has to come much later, for example in the last few minutes of the first session or even in the second or third session when the client feels that the counselor can be helpful.

Example

Client: I don't want to talk to you. My parents are the ones that should be here.

Counselor: Isn't the judge demanding that you come?

Client: Yeah, boy, was he a jerk.

Counselor: I wonder if you can tell me more about the fight you had with your mom.

Client: I told you I wasn't going to tell you anything.

Counselor: I believe you. Let's talk about some subject that you want to talk about.

Client: Like what?

Counselor: You have that Kyle Petty T-shirt on. Do you like auto racing?

Client: Heck, yeah. I watch it every week. Petty is my man. I think his car is so cool looking.

Counselor: It is noticeable out there on the track. Whom do you watch the race with?

Client: My whole family is into it. That's about the only thing we can do together. And that sometimes gets rough if the race lasts a long time.

Counselor: Why is that?

Client: The drinking. They will be drunk if it is more than 4 hours.

Counselor: Do they have a drinking problem or just drink on race day?

Client: Believe me, it is not just race day!

Counselor: I know you don't want to talk about this, but can I ask you one question?

Client: Ask. I don't know if I'll answer it.

Counselor: (*Using a slow, nonchalant voice*) Do these fights you have with your parents have anything to do with alcohol?

Client: I guess I'll answer that. They are drunk a lot. They fight with each other, and they fight with anyone else in sight. The other night I couldn't take it any more. Mom was really yelling at my little sister, who is only 8. I snapped. What can I say?

Counselor: (*Again, using a casual voice*) Ruben, I'm sitting here thinking that maybe, just maybe, there are some things I could help you with, but I'm not sure if you want to talk about any of that stuff.

Client: What do you mean?

Counselor: I know quite a bit about kids in families where the parents drink. I have all this stuff in my head that I wish you had in your head. That's all.

Client: Like what stuff?

Counselor: Are you willing to listen to some information about alcohol and the effects on the family?

Client: Yeah, I'll listen for a little bit. I have nothing else to do.

Counselor: Fair enough. Let me tell you a few things I know about how alcohol affects members in a family.

In this example, the counselor tried to establish a contract and saw that she couldn't. She then worked on rapport, all the time realizing that a contract was needed before any in-depth counseling could happen. She used her voice and choice of topic (Kyle Petty) and words (stuff) to help build rapport, and then she subtly eased back into trying to get a contract. In the end, she did manage to get a contract to talk about alcohol use in the family.

CONTINUING SESSION EXAMPLE

In the last chapter, I introduced the case of Don and his problems with anxiety due, in part, to his relationship with his girlfriend. I presented the rapport phase of the first session. In this segment, I present the contract phase, which is brief since the overall contract is fairly obvious, namely to reduce his anxiety. I spent some time on the specific contract for the session. Also during the contract phase, I explained to Don the **RCFF** model. This is something I do with certain clients to help them understand the counseling process.

Ending of Rapport Phase

Ed: (*In a soft, kind voice*) I think we need to take a look at your relationship. Your love seems almost like an addiction. There is a book on that subject that I'd like you to read.

Don: It feels like an addiction. I'd be glad to do anything that can help.

Ed: Also, we need to look at how you feel about yourself and where good feelings about yourself come from.

Don: I've always worried about what others thought of me. I just don't know what would help me.

Beginning of Contract Phase

Ed: I have some ideas. It seems to me that we need to first work on your gaining some understanding of what is happening with you regarding you and your girlfriend.

Don: I love her so much. I don't know what I would do if she broke up with me.

Ed: Before we talk about that, let's look at the role she plays in your life.

Don: She's everything to me. Maybe I get too attached.

Ed: (*Realizing that there still is not a specific contract*) We're going to cover all of this. What do you hope we accomplish in this session?

Don: I just have to stop feeling this way. I get up each morning and start worrying.

Ed: That seems like a good contract—that is, we will work on helping you to stop worrying. Over the next few sessions, we'll work on helping you deal with your feelings by helping you understand yourself better.

Don: I'm thinking about transferring to her university, but it doesn't have the major that I'm interested in.

Ed: Before we get into all of that, let's first get clear about our contract.

Don: I don't understand what you mean. I just have all these different things that bother me.

Ed:	(*With a caring voice*) I understand that. I want to tell you just a little bit about the kind of counseling that I do, which I call Impact Therapy because I try to make sure that each session is impactful in some way. When using Impact Therapy, I follow certain steps that help me to monitor how the session is developing.
Don:	I'm not sure I know what you mean.
Ed:	I follow an **RCFF** model. The **R** stands for rapport—that's the relationship between you and me. Rapport has to be pretty good before anything else can happen. It seems to me that we are comfortable with each other. What do you think?
Don:	Yes, I'm more relaxed than I thought I would be.
Ed:	Good. The **C** stands for contract, and that is the phase we are working on now. The contract is an agreement between us as to what we are going to work on for the time we meet, and also there are contracts for what we work on in a given session. I think we are clear on our overall contract which is to help you to feel less anxious. We need to decide what we want to work on today. That's what I want us to do in just a second, but let me quickly explain the two **F**s of the model. The first **F** stands for focus, and the second **F** stands for funnel, which is what I will be trying to do in the session. That is, when we talk, I will listen carefully and then try to focus the session on different points or issues and then try to funnel those issues to a deeper level of discussion so that you can gain some insight. Is that pretty clear?
Don:	I think so.
Ed:	I think this will be even clearer as we get more into the session. For now, we need to establish our contract for this session. My suggestion would be that I help you understand the power you are giving your girlfriend.
Don:	I do feel that she has power over me.
Ed:	That's what we'll talk about.

I felt there was a good contract for the session. I was clear that I wanted to help Don understand how he has given his girlfriend so much power over him. I had some ideas of how to focus the session so that there would be some impact.

SUMMARY

Impact therapists make sure that they have a contract before proceeding with counseling. The contract (**C** in **RCFF**) can be either implied or very specifically stated, and the impact therapist will spend as much time as necessary to gain a clear contract. The impact therapist is always aware of the contract since the contract determines what to focus and funnel. Rapport building often takes place during the contract phase because the client can sense the counselor's determination to be helpful. The contract can and often does change as the session progresses. Difficulty arises in obtaining a contract when the client rambles, is confused, has a number of issues, or is forced into therapy.

Chapter 6

Focus

Once the counselor has established rapport and has a clear contract, his next task is to focus the session so that there can be impact. The first **F** of **RCFF** stands for focus. Focusing means taking an issue or point that the client has mentioned and holding the client's attention on that point by using a variety of techniques.

Focusing is vital to Impact Therapy. Clients tend to jump from topic to topic or from one feeling to another and usually do not bring their issues into sharp focus. Over the years, I have observed a number of mistakes regarding focusing a session. Because counselors are often trained so much to listen, they tend not to think of purposely focusing the session. Sessions just more or less drift along, with the client talking and the counselor listening, clarifying, reflecting, and summarizing. These kinds of sessions are usually not impactful.

Therapists who have some issues of their own or who are not able to tune in to their clients for one reason or another may inappropriately focus the session. For instance, the therapist who has unfinished business with his mother or with anger may inappropriately focus clients on their mothers or their anger. Counselors who have been trained to focus mainly on emotions will usually focus only on the feelings when focusing on the client's thoughts, lack of knowledge, or need for training may be more appropriate. Another mistake is focusing briefly on a number of topics rather than holding the focus on one issue. Usually this results in a session that does not go below **7**.

Since clients are often not used to focusing very long on any subject, the impact therapist sees it as his responsibility to focus the session. He thinks about focusing after the first couple of minutes of the session. The counselor is always thinking, "Is there some aspect of what the client is saying or feeling that needs to be focused on?" The counselor has to determine what to focus and then how to focus the session.

WHAT TO FOCUS

There are a number of factors that may be involved in the decision of what to focus. Keeping in mind the importance of focusing, the impact therapist gives much thought to these factors. The therapist has to be aware of the client's need and readiness as well as the contract. Also, the impact path being followed and the theory being used play important parts in what will be focused.

Depending on the Client's Need

Clients often determine the focus in that they come to the session needing to discuss a certain issue. The therapist listens carefully and then tries to focus the session as soon as possible.

Example

Client: I am in trouble. I got caught skipping school, and the principal is going to call my parents this evening. I don't know what to do. Should I tell them before the call comes, or do I just wait? I've even thought about not going home tonight; let them get the news when they are worried about where I am. I could go to Ronnie's, and they would never think to call there, or I could get a ride out of town. This is a full blown mess.

Counselor: Let's try to figure out your best option. First, let's look at the idea of not going home and worrying them. That does not seem like a good idea to me, but maybe I am missing something.

Client: Well, I'm just scared of what they are going to do.

Counselor: Does not going home get you off the hook or just delay their reaction?

Client: I guess you are right. Leaving probably isn't going to do me much good.

Counselor: So now we need to look at your options as far as either waiting until the phone call from the principal or telling them ahead of time.

In this example, the counselor first focused on the idea of not going home and held the focus on that subject long enough for the client to see that the idea was not a good one. Then the counselor focused on the option regarding whether to tell his parents. The client's need was to narrow his options and then focus on the best one.

Depending on the Client's Readiness

There will be times that, although he sees that a client needs to focus on some issue, the counselor chooses to focus the session on something else because he feels that the client is not ready to deal with the subject. There are other times when the counselor may want to nudge or even push the client to face whatever it is she is avoiding. The counselor who is always paying close attention to the client and understands about readiness will usually know when to push and when to back off. It is very important to understand that pushing and backing off are both appropriate and necessary skills of an impact therapist.

Example 1

Client: I had a terrible childhood. I don't even like to think about it. (*Starts to cry*) I don't want to talk about this. It hurts too much. I didn't want to do this—I hate to cry! I am not going to cry in front of you! I'm not!!

Counselor: I can see that it is painful. We don't have to talk about your childhood now, maybe never. Let's come back to the marriage since that is what you are wanting help with.

The counselor saw the need to back off since the client was not ready to get into his painful past.

Example 2

Client: I don't want to look at my family. I have an eating disorder, so let's stick with me and food.

Counselor: But it's not all about food. Family dynamics often play a part in eating disorders.

Client: But I don't want to talk about my family.

Counselor: I know you don't want to, but you need to. There seem to be all kinds of issues with your mom and her suicide.

Client: Why do you keep bringing up the suicide?

Counselor: Because you have too many unresolved issues regarding your mom and her suicide, and I think you have to look at those issues.

Client: (*Starting to cry*) I have never talked about any of this to anyone. It's scary. I'm afraid I'll lose it.

Counselor: (*In a very caring, calm, soft voice*) Caroline, I am here for you. It is okay to let out your feelings. I'll be here. I promise.

Client: I've got so many feelings. (*Client goes on to express many different feelings.*)

In this example the counselor felt that the client was ready and that gently pushing her could open the opportunity for the therapeutic breakthrough that was needed. By focusing on the client's need to let her feelings out, the counselor was able to provide a session that was quite impactful.

Depending on the Contract

Naturally, what to focus on is determined by the contract. Once there is a contract, the impact therapist will try to focus the session on issues that are congruent with the contract. Too often, I have seen counselors allow the session to focus on issues that are not directly related to the contract. These counselors get caught up in listening to the client rather than thinking of the **RCFF** process. They tend to focus on almost anything the client is saying.

By thinking of the contract and focus phases, the impact therapist tends to keep the session from drifting. This is not to say that, during a session, the counselor cannot shift the contract and the focus to a new issue if he sees that it is more important than the one currently being explored. The contract should never bind or limit the counselor but rather should serve as a guide. Any shift in focus should be in line with the overall contract with the client. In addition, the contract can evolve as the counseling goes to greater depth. It is very important to have a clear idea of the contract before there is any focusing. The only exception to this would be when the counselor is having a difficult time getting a contract, so she focuses on different issues to see if there is needed work in those areas.

Depending on the Impact Path

The impact path (chapter 3) the therapist decides to use will determine on what to focus. For instance, if the counselor is being supportive and the client says some irrational statements, the counselor may choose to continue to be supportive by using reflection of how painful the client's life is right now rather than to focus on the irrational sentences. If the impact therapist feels that the client needs to learn basic parenting techniques regarding raising a 1 year old but the client keeps bringing up her guilt about her divorce, the impact therapist would try to focus the client by telling her what he feels they should focus on.

Example

Counselor: Connie, I realize that you have many feelings about the divorce, yourself, and your life, but I do think we ought to stick with talking about basic parenting since you said you are very close to abusing your child, and you don't know what to do with her.

In this example, the counselor had been using teaching as a way to have impact and thus decided to stay with trying to provide the client with needed information about child rearing.

Depending on the Theory

The counselor will focus on different aspects of the counseling according to the theory she is using. The counselor using RET will most often focus on the client's self-talk whereas the counselor using Gestalt therapy may emphasize feelings by bringing past experiences into the present. The counselor using Reality Therapy may focus on the client's plan of action. The therapist using TA will focus on the client's different ego states and how the client changes ego states.

HOW TO FOCUS

There are many techniques that the counselor can use to focus the client. Probably the most commonly used method is asking a series of questions about the issue. Other ways include using different creative techniques like props, writing, chairs, or movement. Below are a number of examples showing how the counselor uses focusing effectively.

Example 1

Client: I don't know what to do with my life now that I'm a cripple. I am not worth anything to anyone! I've been thinking of getting in my car and just taking off so that I won't be a burden to anyone.

Counselor: (*Using a concerned voice*) Are you serious?

Client: Yes, very serious.

Counselor: Why do you think you are not worth anything? Is it because you have a bad leg?

Client: Well, I am used to being very active. Sports, doing all kinds of things around the house, you know what I mean.

Counselor: I understand all that, but still you didn't say why you are not worth anything. Tell me again, why aren't you worth something to your wife and children?

Client: Because I am a cripple—can't you see!

Counselor: (*Using a firm, challenging voice*) I see that your leg is bad—I don't see a worthless person. How are you worthless?

The counselor, coming from an RET framework and using his voice to get the client to think, decided that focusing on the thoughts that led to the feeling of worthlessness would be beneficial. He focused on the topic of worthlessness and would explore the client's thoughts in greater depth unless it appeared that letting the client express his feelings of worthlessness would be the best place to focus.

Example 2

Client: I think I need to talk about my job first. Then if I have time, I can talk about that thing with my brother.

Counselor: What do you want to talk about regarding your job?

Client: I don't know. I just am not happy. I feel a lot of pressure to produce, and I never get any positive feedback. I feel like my whole life is my job. I am working close to 60 hours a week. Some people at work resent that I am there working all the time.

Counselor: Are you expected to work that much?

Client: I am not paid any more. I just want my work to be perfect, and I can't get it done in a regular 40 hour week. I worry all the time that they may come in and something won't be done.

Counselor: And why would that be bad?

Client: I just want to do it right. I am so afraid they might fire me. I constantly worry about losing my job.

Counselor: Let's talk about your fear. Is there any reason to believe you might be fired other than you simply think it? Think about this before you answer.

Client: I sure feel it.

Counselor: I know that. But why? Have they said anything to you to indicate you might be fired?

In this example, the counselor knew the focus needed to be on some aspect of the client's job. He focused the client on one aspect, the fear of being fired. The counselor felt that it would probably be best to work through this issue before covering other aspects of the person's work life.

Example 3

Client: I hate going home. Mom yells at me about everything. It is especially bad if she doesn't have a boyfriend or she is fighting with the one she has. Thanksgiving is coming up, and I am dreading it already. I've got to figure some way to handle this, or I'll be a nervous wreck.

Counselor: Travis, I think what you are saying is that when you go home, you feel unprotected.

Client: That's right!

Counselor: What I want to do is teach you to use a shield when you are home. (*Deciding to use a creative technique to help focus the client, reaches over and picks up a 12 x 12 piece of Plexiglass and hands it to Travis*) I want you to think of this as a shield. I want us to talk about how you can shield yourself from your mom by mentally preparing for what she might say and then deflecting those comments with your shield. How does that sound?

Client: What do you mean?

The counselor used a prop, the Plexiglass, to focus the client on the concept of shielding himself from his mom.

Example 4

Counselor: Wait a second. You're just going on and on about this. I'm going to stop you, and I want to write down your self-talk about how you have to make A's. It is no wonder that you are feeling all this pressure. I think looking at your self-talk can help you to see where the pressure is coming from. You said, "If I don't make all A's, it means I am dumb." (*Writes the sentences on a wipe board*)

Client: Yeah, I don't want to be dumb, and right now I am making a B. I just can't make a B. I don't know what to do!

Counselor: Let's just get the sentences up here, and then we'll go from there. You also said, "If I don't make all A's, I won't get into any college." And you said, "If I don't make A's, I can't be a doctor." Do you see how you put so much pressure on yourself to make grades?

Client: (*Staring at the sentences*) I tell myself those things all the time. What do I do about those thoughts?

The counselor realized that the client was caught up in her negative self-talk. He used the writing of the sentences to slow the client down and focus her on her irrational self-talk.

Example 5

Counselor: Sam, I've got the picture. You are repeating yourself. I want to help you during the time we have left today. You are trying to decide between staying married and getting divorced. I am going to use a chair to represent each of the choices. (*Pulls up two chairs*) Now look at these two. (*Client stares at each chair*) You can't sit in both chairs. You need to figure out which is the best choice for you. (*The client seems to be in deep thought as he stares at one chair then the other.*)

The counselor used chairs to help the client see his problem more clearly. Using chairs to represent different concepts can be an excellent way to focus the session.

Example 6

Client: It all boils down to not liking myself. There's nothing about me that I like.

Counselor: Let me show you something. (*Holds up Styrofoam cup*) It'd be like this. If this cup represents your self-worth, according to you, there are a bunch of holes. I want you to see this. Let's label the holes, and then I want us to talk about what we can do about them. Here, you take the cup and punch holes according to how big of a drain the thing is on your self-esteem (*hands client the cup and a pencil for punching holes*).

Client: My appearance is a big one (*punches hole*). My weight (*punches hole*). I'm not smart (*punches hole*). I wish I had different parents. They are ruining my life. That's a big hole!

Counselor: There are probably more holes, but let's focus on the idea of what to do about the holes in general; and then we'll talk about each one. Go ahead write on the cup what each hole is in case we forget.

Using the cup caused the client to bring into sharper focus her issues regarding herself. She started to think about her different issues. The experience of punching holes in the cup can serve as a reference point for the next few sessions.

Example 7

Counselor: I think what we need to do is focus on the little boy (*pulls up small chair*). This guy (*staring at the chair*) is creating all kinds of problems for you at work; and if you do not figure out how to stay out of that seat, you will lose your job. They probably are not going to give you another chance.

Client: (*Staring at the chair*) You're right. I do have to get that part under control. I am so much better than I used to be. I still hate those four guys for what they did. I'm not going to let them get away with it.

Counselor: And that's going to get you in trouble. We've got to get you to this Adult chair (*pulls up a regular chair to represent the Adult*). If not, it's only a matter of time before you blow, and then there goes your job. I know that we can figure something out that is better than the way this guy is handling it (*staring at the small chair*).

The counselor used the small chair to force the client to see where he needed to focus. The counselor also was firm with the client because she knew that he would lose his job if he did not quickly get a handle on this situation.

WHEN TO FOCUS

There are a number of considerations regarding when to focus. One consideration is whether the therapist should always focus as soon as possible. Another consideration has to do with the amount of time left in the session. Two other focusing considerations pertain to the communication pattern of the client, that is, if the client tends not to bring issues into focus or if the client seems unable to stay on one topic until there is some resolution.

Focus as Soon as Possible

Since impact usually comes as a result of the session being focused, I encourage therapists to try to focus the session as soon as possible. Too often, beginning counselors gather far more information than they need before they try to focus the session. I suggest that the therapist focus quickly but always with some caution since focusing too quickly can result in focusing on the wrong issue or not having enough information to adequately deal with the problem being discussed. Also, the timing has to be right in that the client has to trust the counselor enough to be ready to talk about the subject which the counselor is trying to focus on. Given that the timing is right and the issue is appropriate, focusing as soon as possible is best since it allows for more time to funnel the issue.

Focus When There Is Enough Time Remaining in the Session

Usually when the counselor focuses on a problem or some aspect of a client's concern, it takes some time to work through the issue. It is important for the counselor not to focus on any issue when there is not enough time to adequately work on the problem. If the issue is not very personal in nature, the amount of time will not matter as much; but for some issues, the counselor will definitely want to make sure she has sufficient time to adequately discuss the issue being brought into focus.

All counselors have to be prepared for dealing with important issues that surface during the last 5 or 10 minutes of the session. When this occurs, I usually, after listening for a couple of minutes, make sure I do not start the funneling process since I know we have very little time left. I tell the client that there is not enough time to focus on the issue that is emerging and that we can explore the matter in greater depth during the next session. If I see that this occurs regularly with the client, I will usually mention in the beginning of the session that she has a tendency to avoid exploring her important issues by bringing them up when there is only a few minutes left in the session.

Focus When the Client Tends Not To Bring Issues Into Focus

Often clients will bring up subjects which they need to talk about and then never really talk about them. They tell stories, give excessive details, and express different feelings; but they never actually focus on anything important. Impact therapists are aware that this often occurs; and when it does, they will try to focus the client on some aspect that would be helpful.

Example

Client: The weekend was hard with my stepfather. He is always on my case. Just because he likes hunting, he thinks I should like it. I don't. I'd rather read or work on the computer. Boy, there are some great new programs out now. I like spending hours at the computer. Maybe that's what I should study in college.

Counselor: Would you want to talk about either your stepdad or college?

Client: Maybe. You know, my girlfriend is going to stay home and go to college. I really want to get away from here. She and I are getting along pretty good, but we still fight about my lateness and forgetting to call her. I wonder why I do that.

Counselor: Chico, I'd like to see us focus this session on one or two topics. You tend to go from one subject to the next, and we never delve deeply into a subject. I'd like to see you get a better understanding of your relationship with your stepdad since you will be living with him for at least another 8 months. Let's talk about the things you like and don't like about him. I know you want to talk about the things you don't like about him, but I do want to make sure we also talk about his good qualities as well. He does seem to be a decent guy in many respects.

The counselor decided to focus the session on the stepdad because he felt the topic was an important one. He used his judgement to pick the topic rather than spend another few minutes trying to decide. He felt that the client tended to waste a lot of time during the session, and he wanted to focus the session so that it could funnel.

Focus When the Client Has so Much To Say

There are times when clients will have so much going on with them that they try to cover all the topics in one session. Often the discussion of one issue triggers thoughts about another issue. This can result in the client's not focusing on any issue for any length of time; and, thus, there is no impact in the session. When the impact therapist observes this occurring, he will try to focus the session on one of the important issues so that the session can be productive.

Example

Client: (*In a very anxious, fast-paced voice*) My son was in a bad accident last night. He had been drinking. Thank goodness everyone was okay. I don't know what to do now though. Do I punish him or be thankful that he's okay? Also, this weekend my husband and I are scheduled to go out of town, and we were counting on Jeff to take his sisters to their band practice and soccer game, but now we don't know if we should trust him. I hate to miss the girls' game since it is for the championship. I want to ground him from driving, and yet I need him to drive his sisters. We'd cancel the trip, but my sister is counting on us to come since she just had a baby, and she has two other young ones at home. You know, I am feeling such stress with all of this. This isn't good for me. I just got off medication 2 months ago for my nerves, and I don't want to get like I was. I didn't sleep last night because I had so many things on my mind.

Counselor: You have a lot going on. I am just trying to figure how to best help you. We want to make sure we cover as many issues as we can. It'll be best if we take them one at a time. First and foremost is your physical and mental health. I want to help you figure out what is best for you, given all the circumstances and situations. Let's talk about whether or not it is best to go out of town.

The counselor saw the need to focus the session because it did not seem that the client was going to. He saw the need to focus quickly since there were so many issues to discuss. In other situations, there will be times when the client simply needs to talk about many different topics. In these situations, the counselor will listen, reflect, and provide support and encouragement.

CONTINUING SESSION EXAMPLE

This first session had only been going on for a few minutes. The rapport seemed good and the contract seemed clear. I felt it was important at this point to try to focus the session.

Ending of Contract Phase

Ed: I think this will be even clearer as we get more into the session. For now, we need to establish our contract for this session. My suggestion would be that I help you understand the power you are giving your girlfriend.

Don: I do feel that she has power over me.

Beginning of Focus Phase

Ed: That's what we'll talk about. I want to show you something that I think is symbolic of your relationship. (*I hold up a Styrofoam cup.*) I want you to take this cup. Imagine that the cup represents your psychological worth. (*Don takes the cup and stares at it.*) I'm going to play your girlfriend for a minute. Now, when you got back with your girlfriend, what is her name again?

Don: Jan.

Ed: When you got back with Jan, from what you have said, it seems that you slowly gave your worth over to her. (*I motion for Don to give me the cup. Don does this.*)

Ed: (*Now standing on a chair which is in front of Don*) You gave your worth to her, and now it feels like she can smash you whenever she wants to. (*Don looks up as I squeeze the cup.*)

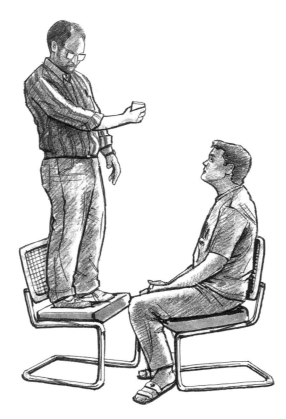

Don:	(*With his head down and in a Child voice*) That's how it feels. I'm at her mercy, and she doesn't seem to understand or care. I am real considerate of her, and she sometimes is almost mean to me. Like last night. She didn't feel like talking because she had two tests. I always want to talk to her.
Ed:	(*Still on the chair*) So it feels like your worth is in her hands and not in yours. Does this feel good, having her up here, smashing your worth?
Don:	(*Looking up*) No! I hate this feeling, but I don't know what to do about it.

I focused the session by standing on the chair and holding the cup. I had Don's full attention and felt that I could funnel the session and make it productive even though we had been meeting for less than 15 minutes.

SUMMARY

Many counselors make the mistake of not focusing their sessions or focusing on inappropriate points. An impact therapist always is considering what, how, and when to focus. What to focus on is determined by such things as the client's need, readiness, the contract, the impact path being used, and the theory being used. He uses theory, props, chairs, and many other strategies to focus the session. He usually tries to focus the session as soon as possible.

Chapter 7

Funnel

Funnel, the second **F** in the **RCFF** steps of Impact Therapy, is the most important phase of counseling because **without funneling, there usually is no impact.** Funneling is defined as taking an issue or feeling to a new or deeper level. In Impact Therapy, I use the ***10-1*** Depth Chart in evaluating how the session is proceeding. I consider any topic which goes as deep as *7* or below as having the possibility for impact. Funneling is taking the issue to at least *7* and then, whenever possible, taking it below *7* to *5*, *3*, or even *1* (see chapter 1). In most situations, good counseling occurs when the therapist pays careful attention to the funneling phase of the session.

WHO IS RESPONSIBLE FOR FUNNELING?

Both the counselor and the client can funnel an issue during the session. More often it is the counselor that creates funneling because clients have a tendency to go from topic to topic, tell long, descriptive stories, or avoid going deeply into their issues because they do not want to experience the pain that may accompany such exploration. The counselor is always responsible for trying to funnel the session when it is appropriate and the client is not doing so. It is not important who funnels the session, but it is important that the session does funnel. Impact therapists believe the purpose of counseling is to help the client gain better understanding of certain issues and concerns; and, by funneling the session, the counselor can begin to accomplish this purpose. The impact therapist is always monitoring if an issue, topic, thought, or feeling needs to funnel.

There are reasons why a counselor may not funnel a session. One reason is that there are times, which I discuss later in this chapter, when it is best not to funnel certain issues. Another reason why the counselor may not funnel the session below *8* is that the client is being resistant to any attempts to go deeper.

One of the biggest mistakes in therapy is not funneling when it would be best to do so. Often times, funneling does not occur because the counselor believes that her primary task is only to listen and reflect. Other times, there is no funneling because the counselor is not following any impact path or theoretical map that takes the client deeper into the issues. Many counselors do not funnel the session because they fear the client's disapproval or are afraid of hurting the client. Some counselors even think the client should be the only one to funnel the session. These thoughts lead to ineffective counseling. Clients should receive the best counseling possible, and too often they do not because their counselor does not understand the importance of funneling or does not know how to funnel.

WHAT SHOULD BE FUNNELED?

Simply put, anything that is helpful and relevant to the client should be funneled. For clarity, I have broken down into four categories what should be funneled: topics relevant to the contract; thoughts, feelings, and behaviors that need further exploration; issues between the therapist and the client; and dynamics occurring in the session.

Funnel Topics Relevant to the Contract

As the counselor listens to the client, he should have in mind what is the overall contract for therapy and the specific contract for the session. If the contract is clear, then he listens for topics to funnel that are relevant to the contract. For instance, if the contract has to do with helping a child understand why he does not like school, relevant topics may include grades, favorite subjects, current teachers, parent's attitude about school, siblings' grades, or home life in general. Irrelevant topics would be about playing little league baseball or the trip to the zoo last weekend. If the contract is to help the client determine if she should move away from home, topics may include finances, social life, family relationships, or family history but not her hobbies or her problems she had in her last love relationship that ended 2 years ago. These topics would be acceptable during the rapport phase, especially if rapport is not developing easily.

It may seem unnecessary to state that one should only funnel topics relevant to the contract, but too often I see counselors funnel irrelevant issues because they are not paying attention to the established contract. It is very easy for the counselor to get off track and funnel topics that she is curious about or that may be very appropriate if the contract were different. A recent case of mine is a good example.

> A couple came to counseling because of marital problems stemming from how very little they have in common and how they do not like doing any of the same things. The woman expressed a great deal of frustration about not ever doing anything. The husband agreed that he did not like to go out much but said that he thought another

problem had to do with the death of their child 2 years before. He felt she never wanted to talk about the subject. I asked a couple of questions and thought about funneling the topic of the death of their child, but then I realized that the contract, which we had clarified during the first 10 minutes or so, was to help them figure out if they should stay together or get divorced. So I asked them if they thought they would have these problems even if their child had not died. They both said yes because of their differences in how they like to spend time, so I felt that funneling on the death of the baby was not going to help them with why they came to counseling.

Funnel Thoughts, Feelings, and Behaviors That Need Further Exploration

Besides thinking of what topics to funnel, the impact therapist also considers funneling certain thoughts, feelings, or behaviors of the client. At any time during a session, the client may share a thought or feeling that is important enough for the counselor to funnel. Too, there are times when the client describes a behavior that the counselor will want to funnel.

Thoughts

One of the main theories used in Impact Therapy is RET, which places great emphasis on the client's thoughts. The main principle of RET is "thoughts cause feelings" (Ellis, 1962). When a client is talking, the impact therapist is always listening for thoughts that may be creating the problem. There will be many times when the therapist will want to funnel a thought so that the client can see how it is the thought that is making him feel the way that he does and that the thought is self-defeating, not true, or irrational.

Example 1

It is ten minutes into a session with a 4th grader.

Client: Amy Jones always makes 100 on her math, and I sometimes miss one or two. I'm so stupid.

Counselor: (*Deciding to funnel the client's thought*) So you believe if you do not make a perfect score, then you're stupid. Explain to me how that is, given that you make good grades in all your subjects.

Client: Well, Amy makes better grades than me, so that means I am stupid. I hate the days we have a math test.

Counselor: It may be that Amy is better than you in math, but I want you to tell me how that makes you stupid. How does Amy Jones have anything to do with whether you are stupid? To my way of thinking, your grades are probably the best indicator of how smart you are, and you certainly have good grades. Answer this question, can Amy Jones make you stupid, yes or no?

Client: (*Thinks for a few seconds*) Well, uh, I guess she can't, but I…

Counselor: (*Cuts in*) I realize there's more to this, but let's first make sure that you realize that you are not stupid. Are you stupid, or do you sometimes not make 100s?

Client: Well, maybe I am not stupid, but I hate to make mistakes.

Counselor: Let's look at why that is, but I want to make sure that you realize that not making 100s does not make you stupid.

In this example, the therapist funneled the client's thoughts by using RET to dispute the client's belief that making a mistake equals being stupid. This session funneled to **6** and probably had some impact since the client was challenged to look at her faulty beliefs.

Example 2

The contract is to help the client understand why she stays in the bad relationship she is in. Here, she has been describing a number of bad incidents with her partner.

Client: …but if I leave him, I'll never find anyone else; so I don't know what to do.

Counselor: (*Funneling her thought*) What do you mean, "I'll never find anyone else"? What evidence do you have to support that thought?

Client: I'm 29 years old with two young kids. Nobody wants that. I was lucky to find Troy when I had one child, so I know finding someone now is impossible.

Counselor: (*Using a voice tone that gets client to think*) Wait a minute. No wonder you stay with Troy. You have thoughts in your head that you believe, but you have never challenged their validity. If you believe that you will never find someone and that no one will want a woman with two kids, then staying with Troy is a good option, especially since you said you have to have a man to be happy. I want to explore each of these thoughts and see if they are true. Let's look at the one that says, "I'll never find someone." How is that a true sentence?

Client: Where am I going to meet somebody? I don't like going to bars; plus, I have my kids.

Counselor: We can talk about how you can meet people, but first let's just focus on your statement that says you will never find someone. Never is a long time. Plus, how do you know what the future holds? If you said, "I'll never be 10 years old again," I would agree, but I do not agree that you never will find someone. Do you believe that your future is already determined?

Client: Well, no. I guess anything is possible; but still, who wants a woman with two young kids?

Counselor: Do you know of anyone who had kids and met someone?

Client: (*Thinks for a few seconds*) Kim Alou met her husband when she had three kids, and Carol Armstrong had two kids when she met Phillip.

Counselor: Then, how can you believe what you are currently telling yourself? You are telling yourself things that simply are not true, and yet you blindly believe them. The truth is it may be a while before you meet someone, and perhaps you may not meet someone; but there is no way to say for sure that you never will meet someone, nor is it true that because you have two kids, no one will ever want a relationship with you. Do you understand what I am getting at—namely, that your thoughts are causing your feelings, and your thoughts are not true?

Clients: They are my thoughts, and they seem true to me.

Counselor: (*In a kind and firm voice*) All of us at times tell ourselves things that are not true and then let ourselves be guided by those thoughts. I am just trying to get you to take a good look at your self-talk and then decide if you want to believe the truth or your made-up thoughts.

In both of these examples the session funneled to depth level of **6** or **5**. The session may funnel even to a deeper level as the client explores more thoughts and feelings that are involved. Very often the impact therapist will funnel the client's thoughts since he believes that changing thoughts brings about a change in feelings and in behavior.

Feelings

Most counselors are trained to listen for and focus on the feelings of the client. **Funneling the session so that clients can experience deep-seated feelings is a very important component of Impact Therapy.** The impact therapist uses a variety of techniques to help clients get more in touch with their feelings.

Example

It is 10 minutes into the first session, and the woman is talking about how much stress she feels. The contract is to sort out some things because the client is unhappy and doesn't know exactly why.

Client: ...and now that I have met someone, my mom is all upset and against me (*starts to cry*).

Counselor: What are your tears about?

Client: Oh, nothing. I cry easily.

Counselor: But what are they about?

Client: My mom (*cries harder*).

Counselor: What about your mom?

Client: She's so mad at me right now. She says I've abandoned her and my kids ever since I met Hank. Don't I have the right to have some fun?

Counselor: Tell me some more about the feelings you are having right now.

Client: (*Seemingly uncomfortable*) It's nothing. She's just mad at me. She is just one of my problems.

Counselor: (*Wants to funnel her feelings and feels that the rapport is good*) Let's stay with this. (*Pulls up an empty chair*) If your mom were here, what would you say to her?

Client: (*Stares at chair and starts crying and in a little girl voice*) Mom, why can't you be happy for me. I'm not trying to hurt you.

Counselor: (*Pulls up small child's chair*) Let me interrupt you for a second. I'm going to ask you to sit in this small child's chair since you are sounding like a small child.

Client: (*Looks at the counselor and smiles, then moves to the small chair*) I feel like a little girl. (*Looks at the chair representing Mom and starts to cry again*) I am just trying to live my life. Please approve of what I am doing. I don't know if I can keep doing this if you don't approve (*sobs*).

Counselor: (*Seeing that the Gestalt technique of using an empty chair has helped the client to get in touch with her feelings, he now wants to start the process of helping her change how she feels.*) Come sit back in this seat, the Adult seat. (*Client moves.*) What are you feeling or thinking?

Client: I do feel like a little girl, and yet I'm 32 years old. I feel so confused about whether I should be doing what I am doing. I feel awful that she disapproves of how I am living right now. And yet, I sure don't want to give up Hank. She really can make me feel bad. Why does she do that to me?

Counselor: Is it true that she makes you feel bad, or do you make yourself feel bad by sliding over to the little girl's seat and then listening to her and to all kinds of negative self-talk in your head?

Client: I guess it is me that does this to myself. I feel so bad when she is upset with me.

Counselor: That's certainly one thing we want to work on—feeling better about how you are choosing to live. I know the little girl feels that she is doing something wrong, but how about the Adult woman? What does she feel she is doing wrong?

| Client: | That's the trouble; I don't feel that I'm doing anything wrong. It's her (*pointing to the little chair*). How do I believe this one (*pointing to the Adult chair*) instead of the little one? |

In this example, the counselor funneled the feelings regarding the client's mom and took the session to a much deeper level. Using Gestalt, TA, RET, and creative techniques, the counselor would continue to work with the client, helping her strengthen her Adult perspective on how she is living.

Behaviors

There will be many times when the counselor will want to funnel on a behavior that the client is describing. Examples of such behaviors are fighting with parents, avoiding in-laws, not talking to people, not seeking a job, or fighting in school.

Example

A school counselor is talking with a student who was sent to her because of the problems he is having in school. It is a few minutes into the session, and the counselor feels the rapport is fine. The contract is an implied one, namely to help this student with his many different problems. The counselor decides to funnel on the student's fighting behavior.

Client:	It all boils down to I don't have friends, I don't like my teachers, and I'm always in trouble for fighting, I...
Counselor:	Let's take a look at your fighting because that causes all kinds of problems here at school. Tell me a little more about that.
Client:	I was born to fight. I like to fight. I like being known as a tough guy.
Counselor:	What do you mean, you were born to fight?
Client:	My mom says I was a fighter as soon as I could stand and fight with someone. She tells me that my dad taught me to fight, before he got sent up. I was 10 when he went to prison. He was a heck of a fighter, and everyone has heard of him around here.
Counselor:	Do you like being in trouble?

Client:	I just always am.
Counselor:	Would you like to understand why that is and how you could choose not to fight?
Client:	It's in my blood!
Counselor:	No, it's something you learned and something that in one way makes you feel good. I'd like to look at the fighting behavior and help you to understand what you gain from fighting and what you lose and where it is probably going to take you.
Client:	What do you mean, gain?
Counselor:	I learned in my psychology classes that all behavior is purposeful, and there is always a privately logical reason for doing something. Often when a person understands his private logic, he then can make a choice if he wants to continue a behavior, especially when that behavior tends to get him in trouble. Do you realize that you can behave differently, still be respected, and stay out of trouble?
Client:	How? I've been this way forever.
Counselor:	I can help you write a different script than the one you are currently following. Your fighting script was written a long time ago, but you do not have to follow the script. It is a choice.
Client:	What do you mean by a script and this choice business?
Counselor:	Just like actors have scripts to follow, so do humans. Humans' scripts are written for them when they are young, and then people live them out.
Client:	I ain't living out no script!
Counselor:	Oh, you are.
Client:	I'm not!
Counselor:	Scripts tell people how to live, and they can't deviate from them. You said you were born to fight, and it's in your blood. If that's not a script, I don't know what is. You can tear this script up (*takes out a sheet of paper and writes on it, "Juan's Fighting Script"*).

Client: (*Stares at the paper for a long time*) I have to think about this. I'd become a different person.

Counselor: Not a completely different person, but different. You have great leadership qualities that could be developed. You also could focus on school and go to college.

The counselor funneled this session to a productive level and seemed to have the youth's attention and, thus, some impact.

Funnel Issues Between the Therapist and the Client

There will be times when the counselor will want to funnel aspects of the counseling relationship because they interfere with the progress of counseling. Relationship dynamics that may need to be funneled include the client being angry with the counselor, the client having romantic interest in the counselor, or the client putting the counselor on a pedestal.

Example 1

Client: ...and I have been thinking a lot about you lately. I like you better with your hair pulled back and in dark colors. I think it does more for your face.

Counselor: (*Remembering some of Bob's comments in the last session*) Bob, we need to talk about our counseling relationship—about what it is and what it isn't.

Client:	What do you mean? I know that it is a professional relationship, but it can be personal too. I don't see any harm in that. Anyway, back to my mom, I did notice...
Counselor:	(*Interrupts*) Bob, I do think we need to discuss your feelings about me and make sure that you see this only as a professional relationship.
Client:	I do, but I think we can become friends and maybe go out when the counseling is finished. That's why I'd like to come more often, you know, to finish with the counseling.
Counselor:	Our goal is to get you to the point so that you are comfortable with yourself, your mom, and women. I am afraid that you are focusing on me partly because I am a woman, and you feel safe with me. The important thing is that you use these sessions to get over your fears, but I sense that you are spending a considerable amount of time during the session and between sessions thinking about a relationship with me, which is not going to happen for many reasons.

In this example the counselor saw the need to funnel the session around the topic of their relationship. Some therapists, because of the discomfort, avoid funneling issues such as these. In the next example, the therapist senses that the client comes to counseling looking for answers rather than coming to think through her issues. The counselor funnels the session by using a creative technique.

Example 2

It is 10 minutes into the fourth session.

Client:	(*In a little girl voice*) I like coming here. It feels good. You are nice to me and tell me good things to try. I like trying the things although I didn't do a couple of the things you asked. Are you mad at me?
Counselor:	No, I am not mad at you.
Client:	Good because I'd die if you were mad at me. I hope you will never be mad at me because then I wouldn't have you to talk to and tell me things to do.
Counselor:	(*Slowly rises and stands on her chair*) Sally, you have me way up here; is that right?
Client:	(*Looks up at the counselor*) Well, I guess so.

Counselor: It is good that you respect my opinion; but if you put me on this pedestal, then in a sense you are having me think for you. You used your parents to think for you, and you wanted to get away from their influence; but instead of thinking for yourself, you now want me doing that for you. Do you want to think for yourself?

Client: I think so, but I don't know if I can.

Counselor: What do you need to do about putting me up here?

Client: I have got to get you down from the chair.

Counselor: That's right. (*Sits back down*) What would it be like for us to be equal and you to use me as a sounding board instead whatever you have me as now?

Client: I felt fear as you sat down. I have always looked up to someone.

Counselor: I know. Let's talk about how you can be your own person and not have to look up to someone. We need to talk about how counseling can be helpful in developing your ability to think for yourself.

Client: (*In deep thought*) This is hard. I don't know that I have ever thought for myself.

Counselor: (*Using a soft, feeling voice*) Stay with that. Say some more.

This session funneled to **5**, and the counselor would then try to get the client to come to understand that she can think for herself. The counselor was aware of the client's Scared Child ego-state and would work to get the client more in touch with her Child part and try to get her to use her Adult more.

Funnel Dynamics Occurring in the Session

There will be times when the therapist will need to funnel some dynamic that is occurring in the session, such as when the counselor is talking and the client is spacing out, or when the counselor is trying to take the session deeper and the client immediately changes the subject. Another example for the need to funnel some dynamic that is occurring in the session is when there is considerable resistance or negativism about counseling on the part of the client.

Example 1

Client: ...so I have spent most of the last 3 days being depressed.

Counselor: Would you like to get some understanding of how you are depressing yourself?

Client: I guess so.

Counselor: I want to talk to you about a simple model that helps to understand where our feelings come from. It is an ABC model. The A stands for…(*Noticing a blank look on the client's face; using a kind voice*) Katrina, you look far away and into yourself.

Client: I'm sorry. It's hard to concentrate.

Counselor: As I was saying, the A stands for the event and the C… (*Again noticing the client's far away look*) Katrina, what is going on?

Client: I was thinking about when my parents divorced. I still remember coming home and seeing Daddy out in the driveway putting his suitcase in the car and then driving off. I didn't hear from him ever again. I never have understood why he left me.

Counselor: (*Switching from funneling on teaching RET and her depression to her feelings of abandonment*) Tell me about those feelings.

Client: I just have always wondered what I did wrong to cause him to never contact me (*starts to cry*). I have always wondered what was the matter with me. I have never felt good about myself since that moment. I think that someday he'll contact me.

Counselor: (*Soft voice*) So you have felt that because he never contacted you, something was terribly wrong with you?

Client: (*Crying hard*) If your father leaves without saying good-bye, there has got to be something wrong with you!

Counselor: (*Using a kind, soft voice*) No, that is not true, but I can sure see how you could believe that. There can be all kinds of reasons why that happened, and most of them have nothing to do with you, but more with him and maybe your mom. I want you to keep talking about this since I hear so much hurt coming from the little girl (*pulls up a small child's chair*) who believes something is wrong with her. I want to help you to see that little girl differently. I sure do.

This session funneled to a deeper level when the counselor realized that the client was not paying attention due to other thoughts in her head. The counselor then funneled what had emerged for the client.

Example 2

Client: I just hate my mother. She is always on my back about picking up, doing my school work, doing my chores, and being on the phone too long. We got into a big fight last night.

Counselor: Why don't we talk about that for a few minutes.

Client: Okay. She's always on me.

Counselor: Do you think there's no way to please her, or do you shirk your responsibilities and disobey her?

Client: I don't know.

Counselor: I think you do know. Do you do what you agree to do and what she asks you to do?

Client: She wants me to be perfect, and I am not. I'm not like my brother, David. He's Mr. Perfect. Sometimes he's disgusting. Can you believe he is 19 and never has tasted a beer or smoked a cigarette? I certainly can't compete with him.

Counselor: Wait a minute. You just switched to you and your brother. What about you and your mom? Let's stay with this business with you and your mom.

Client: She's never on him and is always on me. He makes all these great grades, and then my mom expects me to do the same. Ever since I got caught in that big cheating scandal, I haven't even tried. That was the worse period in my life. I feel school can never be a good place for me. I don't know how I'm going to make it through high school, much less life.

Counselor: (*Still trying to get a contract*) That experience at school seems like something we should talk about.

Client: I beat up on myself daily about it. How could I have done such a thing? That was nearly 2 years ago, and my dad has barely spoken to me since then.

Counselor: Say some more about this.

Client: The cheating was no big deal, but the principal had to blab it all over; and then the newspaper got a hold of it. That's another thing. I want to quit my paper route, but Mom says I can't until the summer so that I can pay for the damages I did to the car when I wrecked it when I was drunk.

Counselor: (*Deciding to focus and funnel on the client's way of communicating during the session*) Abdul, in the last couple of minutes you have brought up a number of important topics; and when I try to focus you on any one of them, you move on to another topic. Are you aware that you skip from topic to topic?

Client: My mind works that way.

Counselor: Have you ever considered if your way is effective for figuring out your problems?

Client: What do you mean?

Counselor: I mean, if you keep jumping around, you can't figure out much. You never keep your attention long enough on any subject to get some new or clearer understanding. What I want us to talk about is not any of the issues you have just mentioned, but rather your ineffective way of problem solving. You are a "touch and go" man.

Client: And you're saying that being a "touch and go" man is not effective?

Counselor: Yes, I am saying that. In counseling, I use what I call a Depth Chart. Let me draw this for you. When you bring up a subject, that is a *10*; and as we go deeper into it, that would be *9*, *8*, *7*, *6*, depending on how deep we get into it. For you, we always go *10*, *9*, *10*, *9*, *10*, *9* and never go much below the surface. I think you do the same thing when you are just out walking around trying to figure things out. I want us to work on your learning how to go deeper into your issues so that you can become an effective problem solver.

Client: So I only go *10*, *9*, *10*, *9*.

Counselor: That's right, and I can teach you how to think more effectively.

Client: Seems like that would help a lot.

Counselor: (*Funneling deeper*) It would. Let's go back and look at how you distracted yourself as you started talking about your mom. How did we get away from that topic?

Client: I don't know.

Counselor: I want you to think about what you did to sidetrack yourself.

WHEN TO FUNNEL

When the counselor decides to funnel a session, there are a number of things she will want to consider. Some of these are rather obvious, such as the rapport, the contract, the client's needs, and the time available. Other considerations deal with how the client is using the session and if the therapist feels the client needs to go deeper. The therapist will usually want to funnel as soon as possible, but proper timing is crucial since funneling often means that the therapist is taking the client to potential emotional pain.

Funnel After Rapport and the Contract Have Been Established

Before a counselor tries to funnel a session, she must have rapport with the client, or the client will usually resist. Also, by having rapport, the counselor will have a basic understanding of the client and, thus, have a better idea of what to funnel.

The contract is important because it determines what, if anything, should be funneled. Sometimes the contract may be to listen because the client simply wants or needs to talk; thus, there would not be any funneling. This is often the case in grief counseling. On the other hand, there are times when the contract may be to help quickly since the client has some urgent need. In most situations, as the session proceeds, the counselor funnels certain issues based on the implied or stated contract between the client and the counselor.

Funnel as Soon as Possible

Since funneling is what most often brings about impact, the counselor will usually want to funnel the session as soon as possible in order to have time for in-depth discussion, exploration, and experiential learning. Once there is rapport and a contract has been established, most clients want their sessions to be productive and, thus, welcome attempts of the counselor to funnel the session. Unfortunately, many counselors do not even think of funneling until the second or third session. Waiting frustrates the client and, therefore, is a mistake.

On certain occasions, the counselor will not want to funnel the session because he believes that the client does not seem ready to deal with what may come up if the session goes to a deeper level. For instance, a counselor may see that the client needs to work on problems with his mother but does not seem ready to face the truth that his mother was and is very abusive. Another example is when the client may not be ready to face the truth about a relationship, so the counselor works to strengthen the client's Adult before funneling to the painful truth of the relationship.

Funnel When the Client Is Telling Stories, Giving too Many Details, or Rambling

There will be times when the impact therapist has focused the session on a concern or topic, but then the client continues telling stories or giving too many details. To make the session productive, the impact therapist will stop the story telling and use any of the techniques explained in this chapter to cut off the rambling and funnel the session.

Funnel When There Is Enough Time

It is very important for the therapist to be aware of how much time is left in a session before she decides to funnel, especially if the issue to be funneled is a highly emotional one such as death, incest, or sexual abuse. In such cases, the counselor will not want to funnel the session because there is not enough time to delve into the issue and bring it to some acceptable closure. In other words, **do not unzip someone if you do not have enough time to zip him or her back up**.

HOW TO FUNNEL

Impact Therapy is built on the premise that counselors need to funnel during a session in order for there to be impact, and there are several ways to do so.

Funnel With Voice

When the counselor decides to funnel the session, one of the most helpful tools is the counselor's use of her voice. **Impact therapists are very aware of the use of voice.** When she wants to funnel a session, the impact therapist most often lowers her voice and slows the pace, which usually has the effect of getting clients to go deeper into their thoughts and/or feelings. Sometimes, however, she uses a confrontational voice to get the client to stop and think.

Funnel by Redirecting

If the therapist has decided to funnel the session, and the client starts expressing something that has already been said, the impact therapist will often politely interrupt and try to funnel the session to more meaningful material. When trying to funnel, the impact therapist will listen carefully to the voice pattern of the client to get a sense of whether the client is thinking or gaining some insight. If it seems as though the client is breaking new ground or giving new information, the counselor will listen; but if this is not the case, the counselor will usually try to redirect the client by using theory, a creative technique, or a thought-provoking question.

Funnel by Very Consciously Staying With a Specific Topic

Often the counselor will need to be very persistent when funneling because many clients tend, either purposely or not, to wander or avoid going deeper. Clients distract themselves, and I have found that many counselors let a topic drift even after the counselors have initially funneled the session. In the example below, the counselor understands that the session is funneling and, thus, avoids shifting to new topics.

Example

Counselor: (*Slows voice*) Let's take one of the topics and zero in on that topic for the next 30 minutes. Which one do you want to work on—your husband's health, you and your mom, or going back to school?

Client: I think my mom. She wants me to come over all the time, and when I do, many times we get into it because she is always worrying about my brother.

Counselor: What do you mean when you say you get into it?

Client: My brother is out of work. He is divorced, and his wife left him with the two kids, Susan who is 8 and Billy who is 5. They are currently living in an apartment with this woman that we all don't like. He really...

Counselor: Let's stay with you and your mom. Do the two of you fight about how she chooses to deal with her son?

Client: Yes, it drives me crazy! She rescues him all the time—she gives him money—money that my husband and I give her!

Counselor: So you want to understand your mom so you don't drive yourself crazy. (*Pause*) I want you to notice the way I said that. We are working on your understanding of your mother and how you are upsetting yourself. Your mom is just behaving in a way you do not like.

Client: I don't understand why she gives him money.

Counselor: Wait. Do you see that you are upsetting yourself?

Client: It burns me up to watch her just throw our money away. Like Christmas, she...

Counselor: (*Lowering her voice, which triggers the client to think*) I believe you do know why she gives him money. Think about it. Why does she do that?

Client: I don't know. (*Pause*) Well, uh, I guess she does it because she feels like she failed him. But my goodness, her life was very hard. She had four kids and a husband who ran around on her. Now my dad, he's the one I am really mad at.

Counselor: We can do Dad later. Let's stay with understanding why your mother does what she does because, once you fully understand, you probably will not be nearly as mad at her. Let's say it is true that your mom feels like she failed your brother and, therefore, gives him money to

Counselor: make up for it. She doesn't want to feel bad, so by giving money, it helps her in some way. Is that right?

Client: I never had thought of it in exactly that way. But my brother needs to get his act together and figure out his own life.

Counselor: That's true, but let's stay with you and your mom. What are you understanding about how you upset yourself about your mom?

Client: What do you mean, I upset myself? If Mom would wise up, I'd not be upset.

Counselor: I'm saying that you have expectations for your mom; and when she doesn't live up to them, you get mad. I want you to look at your expectations and see if they are in line with the reality of who your mom is. Here is the key question: does your mom upset you, or do you upset yourself because of your expectations of her?

Client: Are you saying it's my fault?

Counselor: It's not about fault. I'm trying to get you to decide if your mother is making you feel crazy or if you are making you feel crazy. I believe that if you are willing to get your expectations in line with the reality of who your mother is, then you will understand her behavior, probably not like it, but not be so mad about it.

Client: (*In a thinking voice*) You're saying I've got to quit trying to change her and accept her. It sure would be easier, and I do not like fighting with her. I like her.

Counselor: You're getting somewhere now. How can you not get mad if she gives your brother money or let's him come live with her?

Client: I just have to let her be. She's going to do what she feels best. Do I have to keep giving her money?

Counselor: That's got to be your decision; but if you do, you cannot tell her how to spend it. If you want to, you can buy her things or pay her rent or whatever; but if you give her money, it seems to me that how she spends her money has to be her choice.

Client: What I'm hearing is that I have to quit worrying about how Mom chooses to live.

Counselor: Good point! Say some more about that.

In this example, the counselor knew he was funneling on the mother-daughter relationship, and he kept trying to funnel that topic. There were times when the client brought up other subjects; but the counselor knew in order to have impact, he had to keep trying to funnel the topic of gaining better understanding of her mom.

Ask Relevant, Thought-Provoking Questions

Thought-provoking questions can funnel a session to a deeper level. Beginning counselors often ask questions that lead to stories instead of questions that make the client think. Certainly there are times when the counselor will want to ask information or story kinds of questions; but if the counselor wants to funnel the session, she should use thought-provoking questions. In the following examples, the counselor uses good questions to funnel the session.

Example 1

Client: ...so I don't see any choice but give up the idea of having children since he doesn't want any.

Counselor: That may be the best thing to do, but my question is how much would you resent him if you make that choice?

Client: A whole lot! I'm mad now, and it's not definite.

Counselor: This is a very difficult situation, but is it best for you to give up on something you have wanted since you were 6 years old?

Client: But he is a good man—the best man I have ever been with.

Counselor: (*In a slow voice*) I understand all that; but the question is, is he the best man for you given what you want out of your life and given that you are only 27 years old? I know he wants to marry right now; but if you do marry, then you are giving up your dream. What about waiting?

Client: You're really making me think. When I talk to him, I tend to forget myself. You get me thinking about me, and that's good. But what if I lose him?

Counselor: Let's first decide what you want out of your life and especially the children issue.

The counselor felt that his client needed to think more about what she wants out of a marriage so he consciously funneled the session for a few minutes on that topic. He used thought-provoking questions to accomplish this.

Example 2

Client: I want them to like me, so I go along with them when they are making fun of Tommy.

Counselor: Have you ever thought about Tommy and how it feels to him?

Client: Well, he sometimes asks for it because he does dress weird.

Counselor: So you believe because his family does not have much money, he should be made fun of?

Client: What?

Counselor: I said, "So you believe because his family does not have much money, he should be made fun of?"

Client: I've never thought of that.

Counselor: Think about it. Why do you think he dresses the way he does?

Client: I guess like you said, his family maybe doesn't have much money, and maybe his parents dress funny.

Counselor: Keep thinking about that. What about what you said about being liked? Do you want to be the kind of kid that doesn't think for himself but rather does things just to be liked?

Client: (*Thinks for a few seconds*) No, I want to think for myself. You know, I never really did like what we were doing to Tommy.

Counselor: So what are you saying?

Client: I'm saying....

The impact therapist asked very pointed questions that got her client to think more about his behavior rather than to elicit any additional stories or details. Funneling questions cause thinking and, thus, take the client deeper on the Depth Chart.

Use a Repetitive Question or Statement

One technique that I have found to be helpful in getting a client to go deeper is the use of the repeated question (Passons, 1975). This is a very simple technique where the counselor asks the same question over and over again, with the idea that the client will go more into himself as he answers the question. This technique has to be appropriately timed; otherwise, the client will become very annoyed. When used correctly, funneling will almost always occur.

In the example below, the client had been talking about her habit of eating lots of junk food.

Example

Counselor: Let's do this. I'm going to ask you the same question a number of times, and I simply want you to answer. Why do you eat the way you do?

Client: I don't know.

Counselor: Why do you eat the way you do?

Client: I really don't know. Maybe it's because I like food.

Counselor: Why do you eat the way you do?

Client: Eating makes me feel good.

Counselor: Why do you eat the way you do?

Client: I get lonely, and eating becomes my friend. I sometimes find myself talking to my food.

Counselor: Why do you eat the way you do?

Client: My mom used to always give me food to comfort me when something bad happened—when Dad would yell and scream at me for no reason. (*Starts to cry*) That was horrible. The names he would call me. (*Sobbing*) It was awful!

Counselor: (*After a minute or so*) What are you feeling or thinking?

Client: I think I have always felt bad about myself because of my dad. I never really had put that together.

Counselor: (*Pulls up two chairs in front of the client; tapes the word "THEN" on one chair and "NOW" on the other chair*) Joyce, that was then; this is now. You can live your life from either seat. Which seat have you been living from?

Client: The "THEN" one.

Counselor: Sit over there. (*Client moves.*) How does it feel?

Client: I feel sick. I am so tired of feeling this way.

Counselor: You do not have to sit there.

Client: (*Stares at the "NOW" seat*) It's weird, but I feel afraid to move over there.

Counselor: Let's talk about that because, in order for you to change your life and your eating habits, you will need to move to the "NOW" chair.

By using the repeated question, the session funneled to **5**, with the client gaining new insight about why she eats the way she does. The counselor then used the two chairs to help her concretely see the difference between then and now. The two chairs are very useful in helping clients see that they are living in the past and they do not have to.

The technique of using a repetitive statement is similar to using a repetitive question, with the exception that the counselor has the client repeat a statement a number of times, causing the client to think more about the statement. Again, the timing has to be right in order for this technique to result in funneling.

In the example below, the client had been talking with a boy in crisis over the breakup with his girlfriend.

Example

Client: ...so I don't think I'll ever be happy again.

Counselor: I want you to say that again. Say, "Because Connie broke up with me, I'll never be happy again."

Client: (*Quickly and without thought*) Because Connie broke up with me, I'll never be happy again.

Counselor: Say it again.

Client: Because Connie broke up with me, I'll never be happy again.

Counselor: Again.

Client: (*In a more thoughtful tone*) Because Connie broke up with me, I'll never be happy again.

Counselor: Again.

Client: Because Connie broke up with me, uh, no. I can be happy again. I'm unhappy now. I don't want Connie determining the rest of my life. I feel afraid and alone.

Counselor: (*Using a kind, soft voice*) That's right. Certainly grieving makes sense, but to say you'll never be happy again makes no sense. Let's look at what you have learned from the relationship, what you need to do to get on with your life, and how you want to grieve this important loss.

In this example, the impact therapist wanted to get the client to explore his inner thoughts and feelings. By using a repetition technique, the counselor was able to funnel the session to the client's core issue.

Use Theory To Funnel a Concern

Throughout this book, I have emphasized the use of theory and how it is essential for good counseling. Just as the contract determines what to funnel, theory serves as a map as the client goes to deeper and deeper levels. A counselor usually cannot funnel a session to any meaningful level unless he is guided by theory. In the examples in this chapter, the counselors used RET, TA, Reality Therapy, and Gestalt theories to funnel the session. Funneling the session to 7 and deeper will almost always require the use of theory.

In the example below, it is 20 minutes into the session, and the focus has been on why the client cannot accept money from friends, relatives, or dates who can easily afford to pay. The counselor realizes that the issue is deep seated and, thus, begins to funnel the session to 7 and then to a deeper level.

Example 1

Counselor: (*Thinking in TA*) Do you have any tapes in your head from childhood about money?

Client: I think so.

Counselor: (*Pulls up a small child's chair and places some money in the chair*) Look at the money in the child's chair and think about any scenes or memories about money.

Client: (*Begins to cry*) I remember how Dad used to tell me I was lazy even though I have worked since I was 8 years old. He always said I didn't deserve to have good things, and he made me give him the money I made from working. (*Crying harder*)

Counselor: How old are you feeling right now?

Client: About 10.

Counselor: Sit back in the Adult chair. (*The counselor had already taught the client TA in the last session.*) How old are you actually?

Client: I am 31.

Counselor: Who is running your life regarding money—the 10 year old or the 31 year old?

Client: I guess it's the 10 year old.

Counselor: That's right. What I want us to do is to get the 31 year old to be in charge of the money aspects of your life and probably other aspects as well, but let's stay with money for right now. Say some more about what that 10 year old was taught about herself and money.

Client: I always was told to never take money from anyone or to even ask for money. I had to buy my own school clothes with the money that I made from the odd jobs that I did.

Counselor:	If you had a little girl, would you teach that to her?
Client:	No! I'd teach her that it is okay to ask for things and that she deserves to have things. I certainly would teach her that it is okay to borrow money when she planned to pay it back.
Counselor:	Let's say next week you went to supper with your uncle who is wealthy, and he wanted to treat you to dinner. What would the 10 year old do, and what would the 31 year old do?
Client:	I know what I want to do, but this is hard. I don't feel that I deserve it.
Counselor:	(*Thinking RET and TA*) I want you to challenge this notion about deserve. What does deserve have to do with anything? I want you to think in your Adult and not your Child.
Client:	It is a feeling.
Counselor:	No, it's a thought that you were taught when you were young, and it needs to be challenged by you. How does one deserve to let her wealthy uncle treat her to dinner?

By using theory, chairs, and movement this session funneled to a level where the client gained some new awareness regarding money. The counselor knows that he has to get the client to give up some tapes that she has been carrying around in her head since her childhood. The example also demonstrates how a session can stay productive if the counselor keeps it funneled instead of going off on other topics. Theory definitely guided the counselor to keep the session below **7**.

In the next example, it is 15 minutes into the third session. The client has been describing how his miserable childhood has ruined his life. The counselor sees the need to get the client to try to change rather than blame, which he tends to do. The counselor funnels the session to **6** and then teaches the client RET, using the funneled material.

Example 2

Client:	...and so I didn't have friends because I was too embarrassed about my parents and our house. It was awful.
Counselor:	Garth, it sounds like your childhood wasn't fun, but I think you are now thinking that your whole life has to be determined by that.
Client:	It does. My parents ruined my life.

Counselor: (*Using RET, decides to funnel the client's irrational thoughts*) That is not true. Your parents may have made your childhood miserable, but they are not ruining your life today. Who is in charge of your life today, you or them?

Client: I'm afraid of people because of them! I'm socially backwards because of them!

Counselor: You're partly right in that they did not teach you some things that you needed to learn. But you know what the real question is?

Client: No, what?

Counselor: Do your parents today make you afraid of people and socially backward?

Client: This is how I have been for 33 years.

Counselor: That may be true; but do you have to be this way, or could you learn some things in counseling that could help you change?

Client: I don't think I can change.

Counselor: (*With a challenging voice*) Where is there any proof to that statement? Why can't you change? If you moved to Japan, do you think you could learn Japanese?

Client: I could learn it, but it would take some time.

Counselor: This is going to take some time, but you can learn it. My point is you can learn new things even if you have already been taught something else.

Client: You mean I was taught English but can learn Japanese.

Counselor: That's right. You were taught to be afraid of people, but you can learn how not to be. I'm going to be your counselor, coach, and teacher.

Client: What happens if I can't do it?

Counselor: What do you mean, can't do it? Your fear of people is based on thoughts in your head. What are you telling yourself when you think of going out some place or going to a party in your apartment complex?

Client: I worry that I'll say something stupid, and people will think I'm an idiot.

Counselor: And if someone thought you were an idiot, that would be what?

Client: Just awful. I couldn't stand it.

Counselor: I want to show you how your faulty thinking is getting you in trouble. Do you realize that it is your thoughts that are causing you to feel the way that you do. Let me draw this out for you, and then I want to take a look at a number of things you have said here in the last few minutes. You have said such things as (*listing these on the board*) my parents have ruined my life; I can't change; and if I make a mistake, people will think I am an idiot, and that would be awful. If you tell yourself these things, no wonder you are depressed and afraid of people. These thoughts naturally will lead to fears and bad feelings. Would you agree with that?

Client: Yes.

The counselor used RET to funnel the session and would continue to use it throughout this session and probably the next few sessions. Without the counselor's consciously using theory, the session more than likely would have "drifted" along instead of funneling like it did. The impact therapist also used the analogy about speaking Japanese to help the client realize that learning to think differently takes time and effort.

Use Creative Techniques To Funnel the Session

One of the unique aspects of Impact Therapy is an emphasis on using creative techniques as well as theory. Creative techniques often help move a session to a deeper level because the client gets more involved or issues immediately get clear which, in turn, creates insight or introspection (Jacobs, 1992). In many of the examples throughout the book, I have illustrated how props, chairs, writings, drawings, and other creative techniques are used to funnel the session. Following are some additional examples of the use of creative techniques.

In this example, the client has been describing how tired she feels from all the things that she is doing. It is 20 minutes into the session, and the counselor wants to funnel the session so that the client gets some relief from the stress she is describing.

Example 1

Client: And now with the accident, I am going to have to take Mom to work way across town every day.

Counselor: Lucy, you have got to get some relief. Hold out your arms in front of you. I want you to experience what you are doing to yourself. I think this will illustrate it. I'm going to stack these heavy books on your arms one at a time.

This first one represents being a mother to three young kids; the second is the special needs of your one child; next is working 24 hours a week; next is cleaning your mom's house and your house; next is keeping your nephew on the weekends so your sister can go out; and last is taking your mother to work.

Client: This is too heavy. Can I let my arms down?

Counselor: No. Not unless you are willing to take a good look at your burden and make some changes.

Client: (*Straining*) I can't keep holding them up.

Counselor: Are you willing to give something up?

Client: (*Lowering the books*) Yes, I cannot do all of this.

Counselor: I absolutely agree. You cannot keep doing what you are doing. Let's look at some possible changes with the realization that things do need to change.

The counselor used books to funnel the session to **6** and then proceeded to help the client take a hard look at all that she is doing and how some changes are needed.

In the next example, the client has been talking about her teacher who is always commenting about abortion and how she thinks it is wrong, evil, and bad. The client has had an abortion and feels bad every time the teacher brings up the subject. The counselor funnels this session first about the teacher and abortion then goes deeper (to *5* or *4*) into the client's negative self-talk about herself.

Example 2

Client: ...so I just end up feeling awful.

Counselor: Have you thought about talking to the teacher?

Client: I thought about it, but I hear that Carol Miller did that last year, and the teacher was mean to her after that. This lady is a fanatic. She went to that Pro-Life rally in Washington last weekend. I just have to get through the next 8 weeks.

Counselor: So you don't want to go to her or the administration, but you would rather figure out a way to cope with this.

Client: That's right, but I don't see how.

Counselor: (*Hands client a 12 x 12 piece of Plexiglass*) You're going to need to use this.

Client: What is this?

Counselor: A shield for deflecting her comments. Any time you go to class or around this woman, you have to be ready to put up your shield to deflect her comments. Right now you feel defenseless, but you do not have to be. You can shield yourself. Let's figure out how to shield yourself from those comments.

Client: How do I do that?

Counselor: By anticipating the comments and coming to realize that you made that choice for your own personal reasons and that you are not bad or evil. Why did you choose abortion? Tell me again why you made the choice you made.

Client: I'm a senior and did not want a baby. I want to go to college and then to dental school. The pregnancy came about from a date rape. My parents felt that it was best that I get an abortion. I play on the basketball team and have an excellent chance of getting a good scholarship, and the pregnancy would have been right through basketball season.

Counselor: That's your shield.

Client: What do you mean?

Counselor: When your teacher starts talking, I want you to imagine holding up a shield to deflect her thoughts and see those thoughts you just told me written on the shield. Let's do that—I want you to write those reasons why you chose to have an abortion on a sheet a paper, and then we'll tape them to the shield. (*The client does this and tapes the comments on the shield so that she can read them when she holds it up.*) Now I am going to play your teacher; and when I start commenting on abortion, you hold up the shield and read what you have written. (*They do this a couple of times.*) Now let's do this again, but don't use the shield. (*They do this.*)

Client: The shield is much better. I just have to remember to use it.

Counselor: It makes good sense to use the shield. Do you wear a coat in the winter?

Client: Yes, sure.

Counselor: Why?

Client: To protect myself from the cold. (*Pause*) Oh, I get it. The shield is like my jacket. Hey, I like that. I think I understand.

Counselor: A few minutes ago when you were talking, a question came to me that I wanted to ask you. Do you believe you are good person?

Client: I think so.

Counselor: (*Now using RET*) What do you mean, you think so? I want you to know that you are a good person. The same person you were before the abortion.

Client: How can I be as good a person as I was?

Counselor: Were you a good person last year?

Client: Yes.

Counselor: Were you a good person before the rape?

Client: Yes.

Counselor: Were you a good person after the rape?

Client: That is where I am confused.

Counselor: I want you to think hard before you answer the next questions. How does getting raped cause your worth to go down as a person? How does making the difficult decision to have an abortion make you less of a person?

By using creative techniques, the counselor funneled the session regarding the teacher and how to deal with her. Then the counselor funneled to an even deeper level by getting the client to take a look at her negative self-talk as a result of the abortion. The remainder of the session would funnel on what she is telling herself.

HOW DEEP TO FUNNEL

The logical answer to how deep to funnel would seem to be as deep as possible, but this is not the answer at all since the depth of funneling depends on a number of factors. Some counselors make the mistake of funneling tangential issues and do not give thought to what issues are most important to funnel. Some issues may need to be funneled but only to a certain level so as not to go deeply into the pain. I remember a client I had who had been raped 2 years earlier; and when I asked her about it, she said she would rather not go into it in any great detail, so I just asked her some of the major details and then moved into her current feelings and behaviors. She later thanked me for not making her rehash the events of that evening. The point is that the counselor needs to consider if an issue, feeling, or story needs to be funneled, and if so, does it need to go to **7** where the client gains some information, insight, or new awareness or to **5** or even deeper where the client explores deep-seated emotions.

If the counselor chooses to funnel to a deeper level than **7**, she needs to consider the relationship with the client because the client can be become afraid or angry. Counselors, without good rapport or a contract, sometimes scare their clients by attempting to explore some aspect of their lives that is too frightening, painful, or personal. In the following examples where the rapport is good and there is a contract for going as deep as possible, the counselor definitely goes to very deep levels.

In this next example, it is 10 minutes into the second session; and the client is working on grieving and letting go of the death of her daughter that occurred 3 years ago. She has stated that she wants to get on with her life. The therapist was given permission by the client to push her as hard as necessary to help her heal and let go.

Example 1

Client: ...so I spend a couple of hours a day in her room, for my comfort and hers. It feels good to be with her in there.

Counselor: You are going to have to break that room down and let her go.

Client: I like being with her.

Counselor:	(*In a kind, yet firm voice*) She's dead, and you have to let her go.
Client:	(*Crying*) I don't want her to be dead; she can't be dead.
Counselor:	She is dead, and you have to let her be dead.
Client:	(*Sobbing*) I can't! She needs me. I'm her mommy.
Counselor:	She's dead. She doesn't need you. Your husband needs you. Your family needs you, but you have to let her be dead and get on with your life.
Client:	(*Sobbing*) I don't want her to be dead.
Counselor:	(*Firm, kind voice*) She is dead, and you need to say good-bye to her and let go. (*Using Gestalt therapy, pulls up an empty chair to represent the daughter*)
Client:	(*Still crying; looks at the chair and after a long silence starts to speak*) I'm going to miss you.

This session funneled to *3* or *2* because the counselor had the courage to take the client deep into her feelings in order to get her to say good-bye to her daughter. Using techniques from grief counseling and Gestalt Therapy, the impact therapist funneled the session so there could be impact at a very meaningful level.

This next example is of a third session. The client has asked the counselor to help him get in touch with his feelings since he lives a very flat, uninvolved, emotionless life.

Example 2

Client:	I don't know if I'm ready to look at all that. Maybe it wasn't so bad; and that was 40 years ago, so why would that still be effecting me now?
Counselor:	Our childhood affects us in many hidden ways. I don't think you even realize how bad it was. What are some of the painful things you remember?
Client:	Oh, the hitting and the fights. They were horrible. Things were thrown. I once saw my sister thrown through a picture window. (*Hangs his head and starts to cry quietly*) I was scared all the time. I'd get yelled at for everything. (*Pause, head down*) This is hard. Can we change the subject?
Counselor:	(*Using a soft, gentle, but firm voice*) This seems real important, Carlos. Have you ever talked out loud to anyone about your childhood?

Client: No. I don't like all these feelings.

Counselor: (*Warm, nurturing voice*) It's okay to have feelings. It's okay to cry.

Client: Not according to my father! There was the time...(*Carlos pauses and turns away*) I remember sitting on the couch reading, and he came up and slapped me and said I should be outside. He said I should develop my muscles and not my mind since my mind wasn't worth anything. I started to cry, and he said, "I'll give you something to cry about," and he beat me with a belt, all the time telling me that men don't cry, and he ordered me to stop crying.

Counselor: (*Looks at Carlos, and with a gentle, quiet voice*) It's okay to cry. (*Carlos starts sobbing.*)

Client: (*After a couple of minutes*) I don't think I have ever cried like this. I know I never have in front of another person.

Counselor: How are you feeling now?

Client: Relief. Lost. Not knowing what I should do now.

Counselor: We can sit here which is fine, or we can talk about how this can be a breakthrough for you and how you can start to be a different person than you have been.

Client: Can I really be different?

Counselor: (*With a firm, yet nurturing voice*) Yes, you can. You do not have to be the person your dad said you had to be. In fact, what I see is us working together for the next few months moving you from where you are sitting to way over here to a new seat. (*Places another chair in front of the client, about 8 feet away*) In fact, you have made some major steps today.

Client: (*Staring at the other chair*) I feel like I did take some big steps.

Counselor: You can make it to this other seat. Let's talk about some steps you can make this week before I see you again.

In this example, the session funneled to a very deep level because the therapist had the rapport, the contract, the skills, the courage, and the understanding that the session needed to funnel enough to fully help the client. In the end, by having the other chair represent changing, the client had a very concrete image of what he was trying to do.

CONTINUING SESSION EXAMPLE

This segment illustrates how funneling leads to impact. By using many of the maps and tools discussed in this book, I was able to rapidly move the session along. Don was ready and willing to work, and I saw the opportunity to use some creative techniques and theory. Don was receptive throughout the entire session. I slightly abbreviated the session here since my purpose is to give you a sense as to how things went. Also, at the end of this example, I have provided a portion of the second session and a summary of the third session with Don.

End of Focusing

Don: (*Now with his head down and in a Child voice*) That's how it feels. I'm at her mercy, and she doesn't seem to understand or care. I am real considerate of her, and she sometimes is almost mean to me. Like last night. She didn't feel like talking because she had two tests. I always want to talk to her.

Ed: (*Still on the chair, holding the cup*) So it feels like your worth is in her hands and not in yours. Does this feel good, having her up here, smashing your worth?

Don: (*Looking up*) No! I hate this feeling, but I don't know what to do about it.

Beginning of Funneling

Ed: (*Coming down off the chair*) You have to get Jan off the chair and get your worth back into your own hands. Here, you take the cup, and put it in your left hand and then slowly take my hand with your right hand. (*Don does this.*) That's how you can make contact with her and keep a hold on your worth. There is nothing for her to smash as long as your worth is in your hands. (*I squeeze air with my hand while Don looks at me and then at his "worth" cup.*)

Don: (*Nodding his head*) This is so on target with what I feel. I do feel like at any moment she can smash me.

Ed: We have to figure out how to keep your worth in your hands. How do you get your worth?

Don: Now it is from her. I feel that if she doesn't love me, then no one does or something like that.

Ed: So then you put her above you and then worry like crazy that she is going to smash you. You react to everything she does and says; and if it is the least bit negative or even neutral, you distort and exaggerate the meaning. (*Looking at the chair*) As long as you have her up there, you almost have to worry because you have put her in charge of your feelings.

Don: Right now she is almost my only way to feel good about me since I'm not lifting weights, so I don't get any recognition for that; and I am not spending much time with my friends because of worrying about her and school.

Ed: Another way to look at this is you're a little boy (*pulls up a small child's chair*) trying to get Jan's approval and probably your parent's approval.

Don: (*Stares at the small chair*) I feel like a little boy a lot. I don't think I'll ever feel like a man. Oh, probably when I am 50 or so.

Ed: Come sit in the chair and look up to Jan. (*Don moves to the small chair.*) Is this how it feels?

Don: I hate to admit it, but this is exactly how it feels; and you know what, I think Jan doesn't want me in this chair.

Ed: I'm sure she doesn't. Let's look at this question: How should you get your worth?

Don: From myself, I guess, but I don't know how to do that.

Ed: Do you ever say nice things to yourself about yourself?

Don: No, I don't think I ever have done that. I am very much into what others think of me.

Ed: It's clear to me, Don, that you define yourself by how others define you; and we need to work on getting you to like you for who you are and not so much what Jan and others think about you.

Don: You're so right. Last semester, I wasn't as concerned about what Jan thought, but I wasn't worried either. I've got to get back in charge of my life. I do want my cup in my hands and not in hers.

Ed: I am going to teach you a way to do that. (*I decide to teach RET since Don is going to need a new way to think through his many irrational thoughts about Jan and approval in general.*) What do you tell yourself that causes you to worry?

Don: I don't want her to leave me. I love her so much.

Ed: Let me show you more specifically your self-talk. I'm going to write some of your thoughts so that we can analyze them. It sounds like you are telling yourself things like this: Jan is going to cheat on me; and if she does, I could not stand it! Because Jan cheated on me once, she is going to do it again; and that would be awful!

Don: I tell myself those things all the time.

Ed: Do you realize that these thoughts are what make you anxious?

Don: I've never quite looked at it that way, but that makes sense. I don't know how to stop those thoughts.

Ed: I'm going to explain it's not that you have to stop them but rather challenge the truth of them. Those thoughts are not true! (*I write "not true" above them.*)

Don: What do you mean they are not true?

Ed: I want to look at each of them, but first I want to make sure that you understand that our thoughts cause our feelings. Jan never makes you feel anything, but it is your thoughts that are causing your feelings. The concept that my thoughts cause my feelings is the most important thing that I have learned in my study of human behavior. I truly believe that I cause myself to feel the way that I do. Let's look at your thoughts. Let's look at the second sentence. You say, "Because Jan cheated on me once, she is going to do it again; and that would be awful!" Where is there any proof to that? Granted, she did cheat on you once, but that does not mean that she absolutely is going to again. She may, but no one knows that.

Don: It just seems that way. The only way for there to be proof is if she does it.

Ed: Look at the second half of the sentence, "that would be awful." You would not like it, but it does not have to be awful!! Let's throw in your first sentence, "Jan is going to cheat on me; and if she does, I could not stand it!" There again, you do not know she is going to cheat on you, and you could stand it. You did stand it the first time she cheated on you. Let's write down some sentences that are true that you could tell yourself. (*I look at Don for something to write.*)

Don: I don't know anything different to tell myself.

Ed: I'll help you. We'll take each not true sentence and write it in a true form.

> **NOT TRUE:** Jan is going to cheat on me; and if she does, I could not stand it!
>
> **TRUE:** Jan may cheat on me. I don't have any evidence that she will; plus, we are getting along real well right now. If she does, I won't like it, but I could stand it.
>
> **NOT TRUE:** Because Jan cheated on me once, she is going to do it again; and that would be awful!
>
> **TRUE:** Because Jan cheated on me once does not mean she will do it again. If she does cheat on me, that says something about our relationship or about Jan. I would not like it, but it does not have to be awful, especially if I start getting my worth from myself rather than from her.

Ed: Do you see how you upset yourself by telling yourself things that are not true?

Don: It seems too simple.

Ed: It is, and it isn't. The challenge for you is to make sure you tell yourself things that are true and not exaggerate them like you have been doing.

Don:	This is helping a lot.
Ed:	I'm glad. Tell me how it is helping.
Don:	I realize that I have to control my thoughts. I knew that, but I didn't know what I was doing wrong. What you have on the board there makes it so clear. Too, I have spent most of this semester in that little chair. The biggest thing is Jan being able to smash my worth. I want to think about that some more and maybe talk about it again.
Ed:	Don, I'm sure we will talk about it more. The book and the tape on love addiction will be very helpful and thought provoking for you.
Don:	You know, I dreaded coming here, but now I am excited. I was afraid you might tell me that I was crazy.
Ed:	You certainly are not crazy! I think we can get a lot done in a relatively short period of time. You may want to think of this as a course where there are books to read and things to think about. I would say this course is more important than any you will ever take since it is about you. Don 101.
Don:	I like that—Don 101. (*Laughs*) I hope I can make an A.
Ed:	Why don't we stop for now and set up another appointment fairly soon and then probably go to once a week. Today is Monday; how about Friday at this time?
Don:	That'd be good.
Ed:	Let's stop. I'll get you the book and tape, and then I'll see you Friday.

I felt this was an excellent first session and a good example of Impact Therapy. I followed the **RCFF** steps and was able to funnel the session so that there seemed to be significant insights.

CONTINUING EXAMPLE–SECOND SESSION

To further illustrate Impact Therapy, I have included here a portion of the second session with Don. This session illustrates how quickly we got down to work and how I focused and funneled on three different issues during the session.

Rapport Phase

Ed: How are things going?

Don: I'm feeling much better. I feel 100% better about my girlfriend. It was real helpful thinking about getting my power back. I just kept thinking about that cup. Also, I realize that so much of my anxiety was due to the thoughts in my head.

Ed: I thought I'd audio tape the session and give it to you to listen to. (*This is something I encourage impact therapists to do since usually so much happens during a session; and by taping, the counselor gives the client a chance to listen to the session a number of times.*)

Don: I think that's a good idea.

Ed: Did you read the book or listen to that tape on love addiction?

Don: I listened to the tape. I felt better hearing that others have similar problems. That was real helpful. I read some of the book also. Can I keep it another week?

Ed: Sure.

Don: I'm still having a lot of anxiety even though I feel much better. My parents think I need to work on my anger towards them, especially my dad. Also, I feel a lot of pressure about school.

Ed: Do we need to do more on the girlfriend?

Don: No, I'm okay with it. I think I'm on the right track. I'm sure we'll talk about us some more.

Contract Phase

Ed: Let's work on one of those two things you mentioned, your dad or school.

Don: Dad is mean. He has said many hurtful things to me over the years. We have a business, and I always had to work in the business. I still do when I go home. I resent that he never encouraged me to play sports. Work was always first. There were times he'd go off on me and say I was no good or just to get away from him. He's still that way. I love him, but many times I can't stand him. (*The contract is agreed on by Don's starting right in talking about his dad.*)

Focus Phase

Ed: Are you more upset with the past or how he treats you now?

Don: The past some, but he still bothers me a lot. When I go home, he's often in a rage about the business. He's that way with everyone—my mom, my sister. He says it's not us, but he sure screams at us for all kinds of things.

Funnel Phase

Ed: (*Seeing that Don is in his Adult regarding this situation*) Don, I want you to rate your dad on a 1-10 scale, with 10 being the greatest dad and 1 being the worst dad.

Don: That's hard (*pauses while he thinks*). I guess he's, at best, a 5.

Ed: Does he sometimes say things that are worth listening to?

Don: Oh, yes, there are times he's a decent guy, but mostly he is unhappy.

Ed: (*Pulling up a chair and putting a THINK sign in the chair*) This is you, a 19 year old who understands his dad is a 5, and he prepares for this every time he goes home. He has both a shield and a filter to use when dealing with his dad. (*Holds up a piece of Plexiglass and a furnace filter; Don stares at both of them.*) You need to always be ready to shield yourself from your dad, especially when he is being a 2 or 3. When he is talking, use the shield to deflect the comments. (*I act as if thoughts are coming in, and I am deflecting them with the shield. Don watches intently.*)

Don:	We all need a shield. The man is wild!
Ed:	He's what could be called a rageaholic.
Don:	(*Smiles*) Boy, that's right.
Ed:	Is he alcoholic by any chance?
Don:	No, just a rageaholic. I am going to show this to my sister. She needs it since she is still living at home.
Ed:	(*Pulls up a small child's chair*) The Adult part of you thinks, realizes Dad is only a 5 and will use the shield when you need to. The Child part (*Don stares at the little chair*) uses no shield and ends up feeling hurt and angry because Dad is the way he is. You wish he was a 10 or even a 7, but he's not, and your Adult knows that. It's the Child part that gets you in trouble; plus, there are lots of old hurts whenever you sit in the Child seat.
Don:	It's hard not to sit in that seat. He treats all of us like we're kids.

Ed: It's important for you to realize that only you can put yourself in the Child seat. I want to prepare you for your dad so that you can stay in your Adult. I want to make you more aware of what happens in the situation so that you'll know to use your shield whenever you need to.

Don: (*Looking at the filter in the Adult chair*) What is the filter for?

Ed: What does a filter do?

Don: It filters out stuff in the air. Dust, dirt, stuff like that.

Ed: That's right, and with your dad you may want to use a filter sometimes instead of the shield. The filter is used when you want to let some of what your dad is saying through—that is, the good part. You said that there are times when he is worth listening to.

Don: Oh, yeah, sometimes he's okay. (*Pauses while staring at the filter, the shield, the Adult chair with the Think sign, and the small chair*) This is great. This really helps.

Ed: Do you want to do some more work on your issues with your dad?

Don: No, this helps. I want to think about what we have said, and I'll listen to the tape when I drive home this evening. I'm sure listening to the session again will be a big help.

Ed: (*I decided to focus and funnel another topic, making a mental note to check next time on how things went at home over the weekend.*) What would you like to talk about now?

Don: We can talk about school or about my worries about not lifting.

Ed: (*Thinking that dealing with the lifting issue would probably be a rather quick topic to funnel, and then I'd funnel on school pressures*) What is the problem about not lifting?

Don: I worry that Jan will not like me if I let my body go.

Ed: (*Observing that his body looks fine*) Do you think she is mostly interested in you because of your body?

Don: Yes, I think I do.

Ed: Let's do something. (*I go to the wipe board.*) I'm going to list some characteristics, and I want you to put the percentage you think Jan places on each one. This will add up to 100%.

Body
Personality
Face
Things in common
Other

How much do you think she puts on body?

Don: I think a lot. Maybe 50 to 70%.

Ed: First of all, your body is not bad now. You still are in good shape. Secondly, you think she values your body over personality and things in common. Let me ask, how do the two of you get along?

Don: We get along great. We laugh a lot, and we like doing the same things. We make a great team. We both are into sports and dancing.

Ed: Let's go back to our list. How would you rate those percentages?

Don: This is hard to do because I want to give body a high number, and if I do that, then all the others have to be low.

Ed: I'm trying to get you to see that you are exaggerating.

Don: I'll give you my numbers, but I'm not sure about these. (*Don gives percentages for each.*)

Body	60%
Personality	10%
Face	10%
Things in common	15%
Other	5%

Ed: I think you know your numbers are off. Truthfully, I think they are way off. You're not able to be objective. I don't know Jan, but I know she broke up once when you had your terrific body; and she has continued to date you now even though you haven't lifted for a couple of months. This is a guess. I'd say the ratings are more like…

Body	15%
Personality	30%
Face	15%
Things in common	30%
Other	10%

Don: You're probably right. I am putting too much emphasis on my body. I do want to get back to lifting, I think.

Ed: Don, don't believe my numbers just because I put them up there. The question is do you think mine are closer to accurate than yours?

Don: My numbers are not right. Jan is going to stay with me because she likes me, not my body.

Ed: Don, I hope you do go back to lifting if you enjoy it, but not because you think your body is what is going to keep Jan from breaking up.

Don: I don't think clearly. I sit in that little boy seat a lot. It's not my body that is causing Jan to stay with me.

Ed: I hope you truly believe what you are saying because I think you are right. Do you want to spend more time on this or move to the school issue?

Don: Let's talk about school. I feel a lot of pressure to make good grades.

Ed: Where's the pressure coming from?

Don: My parents. Since I dropped down to 12 hours, they want me to do well; plus, I have an older brother who has a 4.0 in college.

Ed: What have your grades been?

Don: I have a 3.2 average. I don't know that I can make a 4.0 even if I study 24 hours a day. I want to be a physical therapist; and if I maintain a 3.2 or better, I should be able to get admitted to the program.

Ed: Do you compare yourself to your brother?

Don: I try not to, but I do. I wish I made the grades he did.

Ed: (*I funneled further on that issue.*) Is that true?

Don: No, not really. I do not want to study all the time and center my life around grades. I think grades are important, but there are other things to being in college. But lately, I've felt like I must make good grades because I want my parents to be proud of me.

Ed: So once again, you have someone up there (*I look at the chair that is in front of the client*); and your worth is in your parents' hands and, indirectly, in the grades that you make.

Don: (*Looks up at the chair*) They are paying for me to go to college. I should respect them and do well.

Ed: (*In a kind, lower voice*) Don, you are doing well. A 3.2 is an excellent grade point average. If you did not have a 4.0 brother and if your parents did not care about your grades, would you be pleased?

Don: Most definitely! I think I'll do even better when I get into my major. I have gotten a lot out of being here at college. I think all my brother has done is study. I'm not that way.

I end here, having shown how quickly and clearly the impact therapist can work. This case study illustrates how I use creative techniques to enhance the counseling. I continued the session for a while longer. We talked more about how Don puts his worth in everyone else's hands but his own. During the closing phase of the session, Don said that the shield really stood out to him. He also mentioned how the little chair made him realize that he needs to control his insecure Child. He said he understood himself better. He also expressed that he looked forward to listening to the tape of his session and to returning next week.

CONTINUING EXAMPLE –THIRD SESSION

The third session was a termination session since Don reported that he was feeling so much better about everything. He had listened to the tape of the last session a couple of times. He talked with his parents about his grades, so he no longer felt the intense pressure regarding school. He told his mother and sister about the shield and filter. He also talked about how he was spending time with friends again, and he had gone back to lifting weights. He was very excited about what he had learned and was teaching some of the things to his girlfriend.

This is what Impact Therapy is about—that is, helping people as quickly as possible by using a multisensory approach. With Don, I used numerous techniques and theories and provided him with the help he needed in just two sessions. The door was left open for him to return if he saw the need; but by following the **RCFF** steps and by focusing and funneling early in the sessions, much was accomplished in only two sessions.

SUMMARY

The most important phase of Impact Therapy is funneling since most impact occurs when the session funnels to a meaningful level. The counselor is always monitoring if an issue needs to funnel and funnels any topic, thought, feeling, or behavior that is relevant to the contract. The therapist also funnels certain relationship issues between the therapist and client and certain dynamics that take place during the session. Some of the considerations regarding when to funnel include the quality of rapport, the contract, and the time left in the session.

There are many different ways to funnel, including very consciously staying on one subject, asking thought-provoking questions, using a repeated question or statement, using theory, and using creative techniques. The impact therapist gives thought to how deep to funnel, considering such things as the rapport and contract, stability of the client, and the importance of the issue. To funnel to the deepest level, the counselor needs skill, theory, and courage.

Chapter 8

Leading Groups: Skills, Stages, and Phases

In this chapter and the next one, I discuss how the impact therapist conducts group counseling. In this chapter, I discuss leadership style, leadership skills, and phases and stages of groups from an Impact Therapy point of view. In the next chapter, I discuss the use of **PPFF** (**purpose**, **plan**, **focus**, and **funnel**) as the main map for group leading. For a more detailed discussion of group counseling and group leading, you may want to refer to my recent book, *Group Counseling: Strategies and Skills* (Jacobs, Harvill, & Masson, 1994).

The Impact Therapy group leadership model is an active, creative model where the leader leads the group as opposed to facilitating the group as some experts advocate (Carroll, 1986; Yalom, 1985). Impact therapists follow the core belief discussed in chapter 1: **People don't mind being led when they are led well**. Unfortunately, many leaders have been trained to facilitate or play a rather inactive role and thus let the members be responsible for the majority of the direction of the group. This approach does not usually work well in settings such as schools, mental health centers, drug treatment centers, or rehabilitation centers where the members are looking to the leader for direction. More impact can be accomplished when the leader leads the group instead of waiting for the members to lead.

In Impact Therapy groups, the emphasis is on making something happen so that the experience is beneficial for most, if not all, the members. Impact Therapy groups put more emphasis on an intrapersonal experience as opposed to an interpersonal experience. That is, members focus on themselves within a group context instead of focusing on the group and group dynamics. The group is important but not as important as members exploring their own issues and getting help from the group. Members help themselves and each other.

The Impact Therapy group leader takes responsibility for trying to make things happen in the group and, thus, tries to see that each session has impact on many, if not all, of the members. **The Impact Therapy group leader understands that an effective group should be interesting, engaging, supportive, helpful, informative, and insightful.**

The Impact Therapy group leader needs to be quite skillful in conducting counseling in groups and uses the counseling theories discussed in chapter 2 to aid in having impact. She also has knowledge of psychodrama since it a very effective theory for group counseling. For most groups, the impact therapist will plan the sessions and play an active part in directing the work of individual members. To lead such groups, impact therapists use a variety of skills and maps for guiding themselves as they lead.

SKILLS OF AN IMPACT THERAPIST

Many skills, such as listening, summarizing, questioning, clarifying, and encouraging, are necessary for leading impactful groups. The leader also needs to be able to set a positive tone, use her voice and eyes effectively, and effectively begin and end the sessions. The following skills are also essential because the impact therapist knows it is his responsibility to try to make the group experience valuable for everyone.

Cutting Off

The most needed skill for leading effective Impact Therapy groups is the ability to interrupt because the leader is the person who makes sure that meaningful dialogue takes place. In any group, members tend to go off on tangents, talk all at once, ramble, or switch subjects. To provide a valuable group experience, the leader has to know how to skillfully cut off the members in order to focus and funnel the session on meaningful topics or on members who want to work through pertinent issues. I tell members during the first session that I will, at times, interrupt what is happening in order to allow more members to get involved in the discussion, switch to another topic, or keep the focus on a current topic. I explain that one of my roles is to make sure that we stay on track and that no one member dominates the discussion. I also explain that because I am the leader, I am thinking about every member and how best to use the group's time. Many leaders do not cut off for fear of hurting members' feelings. These leaders fail to realize that they are hurting other members because valuable time is being wasted, and the members often are bored when nonproductive dialogue takes place.

There are three notable situations where the leader needs to interrupt: when the group is staying at the *10*, *9*, *8* level on the Depth Chart and not funneling to any meaningful level; when a member is working on some issue but is not going below *7*; and when a member switches the focus or is starting to express something that will be counterproductive.

Cutting off when the group is at the 10, 9, 8 level

Very often, discussion in groups starts at a superficial level and continues the entire session unless the leader focuses and funnels the group. In the examples below, the leader intervenes and tries to funnel the session because the members are not engaging in any meaningful discussion.

Example 1

Lori: I can't decide if spanking is okay or not. My husband definitely thinks it is, but I'm not sure. I heard a speaker at church say that spanking models violence. I'd never thought of it that way.

Brooke: I was sure afraid of my dad and his spankings. Mom would always say, "Wait until your dad gets home, little girl!" He'd spank me, and I'd try my best not to cry.

Nancy: I was just the opposite. I'd cry before I got the spanking so that they would not spank me. That worked a lot of the time.

Julie: I wish I'd thought of that. When I...

Leader: (*Seeing the need to focus on spanking in a more meaningful way, interrupts, using a soft, thinking voice*) Julie, let me jump in here and try to take this to a deeper level because this is an important issue. I want each of you to think about what you believe about spanking and why. Also, think if your behavior and beliefs are congruent. I think this is a very important concept, and I want you to think about what Lori said she heard at her church— that spanking models violence.

Example 2

Jane: I'd like to talk about the holidays coming up and how to not drink at all the parties and things. That seems like it is going to be hard.

Brian: That's true. My brother has this great party that goes until all hours of the morning. The only way for me to not drink is to not go.

Dave: That seems so unfair. We have to have a life. We can't avoid alcohol all our lives.

Jane: There are three big parties that I have to decide about. One is going to be at the hotel for all the business owners in town, and then there's one at my in-laws that is huge, and then one in our neighborhood.

Alan: I have four that I know of. One is...

Leader: (*Seeing that the members are staying on the surface and are not focusing on any important issues, decides to interrupt*) Alan, let me interrupt here. This is a good topic—what to do about parties. I want each of you to think about how you are going to handle the holidays and different parties. First, think about if you are going to go to the party and why. Then I want you to think about how you are going to handle being around so many people who are drinking. (*Pause*) Let's look at whether you are making a good decision by going.

Cut off and stay with the member when he or she is not going deeper

If a member is talking superficially, rambling, repeating a story, or telling a story in too great of detail, the impact therapist will intervene and try to focus and funnel the session. The first thing she considers is whether to cut and stay with the person or focus elsewhere. The leader has many ways to cut off and stay with the person. By cutting and staying, I mean that the leader cuts off the member but keeps the focus of the group on that member. When the leader decides to cut and stay with a member, she has to decide if she wants the member to keep talking, only on a different level, or if she wants to involve other members. The examples below show both ways of cutting and staying. In each of these examples, I start with the "leader interrupts" to indicate that the leader does not sit politely waiting for the member to finish because far too often the member will go on too long, wasting valuable time. Also, when cutting off, the leader uses a kind but firm voice.

Example 1

Leader: (*Interrupts member*) Trina, let me stop you. If we work with you for the next 20 minutes, what help do you want? How can the group be helpful?

Trina: I'm not sure.

Leader: I think that's right, so you more or less are going in circles. I want you to think about what it is that you want help with.

The leader interrupted because he felt that Trina was going in circles and not focusing or funneling. The leader cut off Trina but kept the focus on her. This forced Trina to stop and think about what she wanted. It also alerted Trina to the fact that she only had a certain amount of time to work on her issue.

Example 2

Leader: (*Interrupts because member is not funneling deeper; using a kind, thinking voice*) Jana, I'm going to ask you to stop. (*Turns to members*) I want you to think of a question that you want to ask Jana about her situation that you believe will make her have to think more about it. (*Looking at Jana*) I'm doing this because you tend to just describe the situation, and I feel you need to dig deeper. Hopefully, our questions will cause you to really think about your situation.

In this group, the leader cut off and stayed with the member by having other members ask questions. This often causes the member to focus and funnel because she has to answer questions rather than tell stories that she has often rehearsed. The leader will listen for good questions and also will listen carefully to Jana to hear if she is using a thinking voice as she answers. If the members were not able to ask good questions, the leader would start out. Usually one or two members would then have good questions to ask. If the member is not thinking, the leader would point that out since the whole purpose is to get her to think.

Often the leader will see the need to cut off and get the member to think more about what she is saying. The impact therapist may use different props, as in the examples below, to focus the members.

Example 1

Leader: (*Using a kind, firm voice*) Matt, stop for a minute. (*Pulls small chair in front of Matt*) Do you realize that your Child part is the one causing all the problems? (*Matt looks at chair and then looks puzzled; leader turns to the group.*) Do you see the problem as coming from Matt's Child? (*Heads nod.*) Matt, I'm going to come back to you, but I want each of you to think how your Child gets in the way in your current relationships. (*All are staring at the chair.*) It's easy to see the Child in others but not in ourselves. Matt, what are you thinking?

The leader used the chair to interrupt and focus Matt and also to engage the other members. The impact therapist tries to get members to think about their issues, and the use of props often focuses not only the working member but also the other members. The prop gives everyone a focus point.

Example 2

Leader: (*Using a kind, warm voice*) Kathy, we have heard this before. (*Holding up a cassette tape*) It's like you are playing a tape for us. (*Turns to the group*) Would all of you agree that we have heard this before? (*Heads nod.*) Instead of telling us more stories, I think we would all like to hear you talk about what you want to do about your situation. (*Looking at Kathy*) We'd like to help you make a new tape that has you telling yourself positive things and doing something about your situation. (*Holding up a tape that is new*)

The leader has skillfully cut off and focused Kathy and the other members on the idea of making new tapes instead of playing the old ones. The leader stayed with Kathy and tried to get her to think of new things to do and tell herself.

Example 3

Leader: *(Realizing that the member is going over the same thing as last week and is not funneling, and members are starting to get bored)* Roy, I want to try something different. *(Turns to the group)* I want all of you to look at me, and we are going to discuss Roy and his situation regarding his wife's affair, the baby, and the other guy. What do you think Roy needs to do with all this? Look at me and not at Roy.

Vicki: I think Roy hasn't really accepted the whole thing. Sure, it is a tough thing; but if he is going to stay with Connie, then he cannot keep badgering her. *(Roy is listening very intently.)*

Jerry: That's right. They are bound to fight, the way he is acting.

Leader: What ego state do you think Roy is coming from?

Vicki: Most definitely his Child. He has to get an Adult perspective on this, or everyone is going to suffer forever.

Leader: Who can play an Adult ego state dealing with this set of facts?

Ivan: I think I can. My wife had an affair. Now granted, there was no baby, but still I think it is similar. Do you want me to try?

Leader: *(Pulls up a small chair and a regular chair; Roy stares at the chairs.)* Ivan, come sit in the Adult chair.

In this example, the leader cut off and stayed with Roy in a different way. He had Roy listen rather than talk because the leader felt that when Roy talked, he often did not think; so the leader decided to let Roy hear the other members' thoughts about the situation.

There are many other ways to cut and stay with a member, but the point that I want to emphasize is this: **the impact therapist understands that it is her responsibility to cut off and try to focus and funnel a member who is not going below 7 on the Depth Chart**. So often, members talk at the *10*, *9*, *8* level, and the leader does not intervene which results in a nonproductive and boring group experience.

Cut off and leave the member but stay with the topic

One option the leader has when cutting off is to leave the member but stay with the topic. This allows that particular member to continue to think about what he was saying while getting other members involved. The member does not usually feel cut off.

Example

Leader:	*(Interrupts member who had been going on about his responsibility for his parents' divorce. Earlier when the counselor tried to funnel the member, he avoided funneling and told another story.)* Rajal, I want to pick up on this idea of blaming yourself for your parents' divorce. Do others of you believe that you caused your parents' divorces?
Heather:	*(Head down, crying)* I definitely do. My mom said it was my fault because I made her hit me, and then Daddy took up for me.
Leader:	Let's hear from the rest of you then. Heather, we'll come back to you.

The leader left Rajal but stayed with Rajal's topic of blaming oneself for the divorce. He decided to focus on Heather, but first he wanted everyone to comment since he knew that the issue of blame was an important one to discuss.

Cut off and leave the member and the topic

There will be times when the leader will decide to cut off the member and go to another topic. This may be done for any number of reasons including the current topic's not being relevant, the leader's seeing that greater benefits would come from discussing something different, the leader's wanting to introduce a group exercise, or the leader's needing to start the closing.

Example

Kevin:	You think your boss is bad, let me tell you about mine! The other day my boss changed her mind three times within one hour regarding whether I should start this big project. She first told me not to start it because of the back orders that we had. Then she...
Leader:	I think we need to shift our focus. A number of you have legitimate complaints about your boss, which is one source of stress. Let's look at all the different ways you experience stress at work, and then we'll talk about what, if anything, can be done.

Being able to skillfully cut off is absolutely necessary for leading Impact Therapy groups. The group leader has to be able to stop any member from dominating the group or taking the group on irrelevant tangents. In all of the examples above, the impact therapist saw that he needed to cut off in order to make the group more impactful.

Drawing Out

Members in a group should not be allowed to sit quietly and never talk. It is not good for the overall group dynamics, nor is it good for the quiet person, unless there is a very good reason why the person acts the way he does. Certainly some members will talk much more than others, and some will not want to say very much; but it is the responsibility of the leader to try to draw out the quiet members. There are a number of different ways for drawing out quiet members in a group.

Sentence completions

Sentence completion exercises consist of having members complete a list of three or five incomplete sentences about some topic, such as parenting, stress, school, or divorce. The leader then can call on the different members to read what they wrote; most members usually feel comfortable sharing their answers.

Other writings

By having members list, check off, rate, or write a definition or paragraph on a particular subject, the leader can call on members to share what they wrote. Most members do not feel put on the spot as long as they have something in front of them to read. By having the quiet member share, the leader can get some idea of what the person is thinking and can ask him to say more about his list, rating, or definition.

Rounds

The round is an exercise where the leader asks everyone to comment on something, such as "In a word or phrase, how was the week?" or "On a 1-10 scale, with 10 being very comfortable, how would you rate your comfort in the group?" (I discuss rounds in detail in chapter 9.) Rounds are good for drawing out because most members will share a word or number, and then the leader or other members may ask them to say more.

Dyads

Sometimes when there are quiet members, the leader can use dyads or pairs as a way to get members to talk. Most members will talk if they are paired with another member. In some situations, the leader can pair herself with the quiet member and ask him why he does not talk in the large group. If the leader shows she cares and is concerned, often the member will give her permission to comment to the rest of the group on why he is not sharing. This, in turn, usually will lead to a discussion with the quiet member joining in and sharing.

Gentle nudging

I use this phrase to describe how the leader can encourage the quiet member to talk. Some leaders make the mistake of calling on the member who, consequently, feels put on the spot. I suggest calling on the member, maintaining brief eye contact, then calling on another, so that two people have been called on.

Example

Leader: (*Using a gentle, encouraging voice; looking at Pat*) Pat, you have not said how it is in your family. (*Seeing that Pat doesn't seem eager to talk; after a few seconds*) Or Terri, do you want to comment? (*Leader looks at both Pat and Terri to see if either wants to talk.*)

In this example, the leader encouraged Pat and Terri to talk by calling on them; but if neither wanted to talk, he would move on by asking another, more vocal member to comment. Often the gentle nudge helps the quiet member to comment while not putting a whole lot of pressure on the member to speak.

All the techniques above are useful when the leader has members that do not tend to share. The important thing to remember is that it is usually best to have members contribute some during each session because one of the purposes of most groups is learning to be comfortable sharing with others.

Generating Interest

Impact therapists believe that one of their tasks as group leaders is to generate interest in the group by bringing up interesting and relevant topics. The impact therapist generates interest by introducing creative and thought-provoking exercises. She also creates interest by funneling the session below **7**. For most members, a session that funnels below **7** will be interesting. Chapter 9 includes several examples of how the impact therapist generates interest.

MAPS FOR GUIDING A GROUP

Because leading groups is such a complex task, having different maps for guidance is quite helpful. I use the term map to refer to a concept or mental image that helps the leader to know what is happening in the group. Although the primary map for leading an impact therapy group is **PPFF** (discussed in chapter 9), below I discuss briefly two additional maps which can be found in most group counseling literature: Stages of the Group and Phases of a Session.

Stages of the Group

Every group that meets for a number of sessions goes through stages, and it is important for the leader to be aware of the stage of the group. All groups go through beginning, working, and ending stages (Corey, 1990; Jacobs, et al., 1994). The beginning stage can take as little as a few minutes during the first session or as much as two or three entire sessions, depending on the members and the purpose of the group. In the beginning stage, the members are getting comfortable with themselves, the other members, and the leader, as well as with the content or purpose of the group. The impact therapist pays much attention to the beginning stage since it sets the tone for the remaining sessions.

The impact therapist plans carefully the initial minutes of the beginning stage, considering the purpose of the group, how she'll introduce herself, and how members will be introduced to each other. During the beginning stage, the leader is aware that members are learning how to be in the group, so she makes sure that no members dominate the group and that everyone gets involved, if at all possible. The leader also gives thought to what would be interesting and appropriate to discuss during the beginning stage, realizing that some topics will be more appropriate than others. It is also during this stage that the leader clarifies her role.

The working stage of the group is the period during which valuable discussion and personal exploration takes place. This stage occurs whenever the members seem to be comfortable sharing and working on the group's purpose. The impact therapist tries to get her group to the working stage as soon as possible (usually by the second session, possibly during the first) because it is at this stage that impact takes place. The leader will often plan the sessions based on the comfort level and needs of the members.

The closing stage is the time when the group is ending—where members are sharing what the experience has meant to them and what is next for them. Leaders spend either one or two sessions or part of the last session closing a group. The amount of time depends on how important the group has been in the members' lives. For groups that have been very impactful, such as some therapy or support groups, a longer closing is needed. During the closing stage, the skilled leader will get the group to engage in summarizing and finishing with each other rather than working on new material.

Phases of a Session

There are three phases to any session: *the warm-up or beginning phase, the middle or working phase,* and *the ending or closing phase* (Jacobs, et al., 1994). The Impact Therapy group leader is always aware of what phase the session is in since the leader does different things in each of the phases.

During the beginning phase, any new members are introduced, and members are warmed up for the middle phase. Often in the beginning phase, members give progress reports on things that they have been working on and share how their lives have been going. The impact therapist pays careful attention during this phase to make sure it does not last too long because there is usually very little impact during the warm-up phase. One mistake that is often made is allowing members to discuss irrelevant topics or letting members tell long, detailed stories. The impact therapist knows that she may need to use her cut-off skills during this phase.

The middle or working phase is the part of the session when the group leader tries to have impact by focusing and funneling on issues, topics, or members. This phase should comprise the majority of time of any given session except for perhaps the first and last sessions. The impact therapist pays attention to the depth of the discussion during this phase and tries to funnel the session below 7 on the Depth Chart whenever possible. By always thinking about the depth of the session, the impact therapist tends to lead groups that are impactful and interesting. That is, whenever the group is not below 7 and is more or less drifting, the impact therapist uses different group leadership skills, group exercises, and creative techniques to focus and funnel the session.

The Impact Therapy group leader believes that it is her responsibility to make sure that the group is productive and valuable for as many members as possible. It is during the middle phase that the leader sometimes has to appropriately and skillfully cut off members, draw out members, introduce significant exercises, facilitate meaningful discussions on various topics, and generate work on personal issues.

The ending phase should be the time when the leader closes the group. It is important to allow time for this phase so members can have closure on the session. During this phase the leader or members may summarize the session, comment on what they learned, offer wishes for other members, or discuss what topics they want to focus on at the next meeting. The leader usually does not focus or funnel any issue that comes up during this phase which needs some time to discuss. I say this because there is sometimes a tendency for members to wait until the last few minutes to bring up important issues. This does not happen very often in an Impact Therapy group because the leader consciously tries to draw issues out during the middle phase.

SUMMARY

Impact Therapy believes in an active approach to group leading. Three very important skills of an Impact Therapy group leader are cutting off, drawing out, and generating interest and energy. The impact therapist uses different maps to guide her in her groups. One map is the three stages of groups: the beginning, working, and closing stages. Another map is the phases of the session, which are the warm-up, middle or working, and ending phases. Paying attention to these maps helps to guide the active leader in developing an impactful group experience.

Chapter 9

Leading Groups: Purpose, Plan, Focus, and Funnel

An impact therapy group leader uses **PPFF** (**purpose**, **plan**, **focus**, and **funnel**) as the main map for effective group leading. If a leader pays attention to **PPFF**, she should have a good group experience, given that the leader has some say in the composition of the group. In earlier chapters, I discussed in detail the terms Focus and Funnel as they relate to individual counseling; in this chapter, I discuss these terms as they relate to group leading. I also introduce two other key components of group leading: Purpose and Planning.

PURPOSE

The key to good group leadership is clarity of purpose on the part of the leader. By purpose, I mean the intent, goal, or reason for meeting. The leader must know the purpose before recruiting members and before leading any session because the reason for meeting determines the size and kind of group and type of member, as well as the kind and the depth of sharing. For instance, a parent education group is conducted very differently from a parent support or parent therapy group. In a parent education group, the leader is providing information and facilitating discussion, whereas in a support or therapy group, the leader tries to get the members to share and often to focus in-depth on one person or topic.

The purpose determines the content, and the impact therapist is responsible for making sure that the content is relevant to the purpose. In a men's support group, discussing politics, movies, or sports would not be relevant, whereas pressures about money, what it means to be a man, and sexual performance would be content that is very much in line with the purpose. If a group in a prison has as its goal improving communications with family members, then complaining about the food or the warden would be inappropriate. In a rehabilitation center where the intent of the group is to help members adjust, discussing at length each person's medical condition would not be congruent with the purpose.

The impact therapist is always clear as to the purpose of any group or session he leads. For example, during the first session of a personal growth/therapy group, the leader understands that the overall purpose of the session is to get the group off to a good start. One goal is to clarify the group's purpose and to help members get comfortable. Another goal is to focus on one or two relevant topics so that members get an idea of what will be discussed and how the group will be conducted. During the working stage of this group, the leader may plan sessions on any of the following topics: sex, money, parents, religion, work, and children. By having a clear purpose for the session, the leader tends to keep the group focused which, in turn, brings about more impact.

Many leaders fail to be clear as to their purpose and let their groups go where ever they go. When this occurs, the members often are frustrated because the group tends to go in many different directions rather than staying focused in one direction. Leaders who do not have a clear purpose often lead groups that go *10*, *9*, *8*, *10*, *9*, *8*, *10*, *9*, *10*, *9*, *8*, *10*, *9* on the Depth Chart whereas leaders with a purpose funnel the group below *7*. The leader who clearly understands the purpose of the group will prevent the members from wandering far from relevant subjects. Also, clarity causes the leader to meaningfully focus and funnel the session. **Clarity of purpose is absolutely essential for leading a good group.**

PLAN

Good planning is necessary for all groups since members may come to a session and have no pressing issues they want to bring up. Also, once the leader knows the members, he can think of activities that would help them work on their issues. Purpose and planning go together because no planning can be done without the purpose in mind, and the purpose cannot be met if there is no planning.

Even before the first session, the impact therapist engages in what I call "big picture" planning, which is listing the issues or topics that would be relevant for the given purpose of the group. I encourage leaders to write these topics down so that they have a general idea of what should be discussed during the life of the group. Once this is done, the leader then considers if there needs to be an order to when the topics should be discussed. By doing this kind of planning, the leader is prepared to either deal with the topic, explain to the group that it will be dealt with later, or explain that the topic is not in line with the general purpose.

An example of big picture planning for an Adult Child of Alcoholics group would include the following topics (not in any order of importance or when they should be brought up in group):

Shame

Anger

Attitude toward drinking parent

Attitude toward nondrinking parent

Trust (ability to share)

Fun

Intimacy

Role one played in the family

Blame

Self-esteem

Ability to nurture oneself

Size of the different ego states

Lying

Current attitude toward drinking

Parenting differently or parenting the same (if members
   have children)

Relationship with siblings

By engaging in this kind of planning, the leader begins to clarify in her mind the purpose of the group and the many different topics that can and should be covered. Because the Impact Therapy group leader is very active and takes responsibility for making the group relevant and meaningful, big picture planning is imperative.

For some groups, once the big picture is planned, the leader can plan the sessions for the entire life of the group. Some personal growth groups, communications groups, topic groups, and skills groups can be planned in their entirety because they have a developmental order to them. However, for most groups, because planning is based in part on what happened during the last session, the leader plans before each session rather than plans the entire series of sessions.

Planning a Session

When planning, the leader always considers the stage of the group and each phase of the session. First, the leader plans how she is going to conduct the warmup. This is especially important for the first two or three sessions of a group since the members are still getting used to the experience of being in a group. For most groups, the leader also plans the middle phase, giving thought to what topics would be good to focus on and how to focus the session. Group exercises are often used to focus the session. However, for therapy and support groups, where members bring up issues, the middle phase cannot be planned except for giving much thought to possible issues that may arise. Also, the leader should have a back-up plan (relevant and interesting topics) in the event members do not have any issues they want to discuss. I never lead any support or therapy group where I have not given thought to at least a couple of topics that I think would be interesting for the members. I also have a couple of exercises in mind that would be helpful to introduce relevant topics.

The ending phase should also be planned in that the leader gives thought to how he is going to close the session. The leader should consider the amount of time that he thinks will be necessary for closing and whether he wants to use dyads, rounds, wishes, or comments. He should also consider if there needs to be discussion about the topic for the next session and if some kind of homework for next week would be valuable.

Even though I emphasize the importance of planning, I do not encourage or even suggest that a leader stick rigidly to the plan. Being flexible is a sign of a good leader. Good planning provides structure and confidence for an impactful session yet leaves room for flexibility if the situation calls for a change. I suggest leaders deviate from the plan if the new direction is relevant to the purpose and the new direction is equal to or better than the direction that the leader had planned. Also, I suggest that leaders go with the new direction *only* if they have some good ideas of how to focus and funnel the new topic or issue.

Sample Plans

When planning a session, the impact therapist writes out in some detail the activities and topics during each phase and also estimates the amount of time for each activity. Too often, leaders who do not plan according to time let far too much time pass on one issue and, thus, never get to some other and often more important issues. Below is one leader's plan for the first session of a six-member alcohol recovery group.

<u>Warm-up Phase</u>

    2 minutes—Introduce self and welcome people to the group

    2 minutes—Introductions—name, amount of time in recovery, and a word or phrase about how they are feeling about being in the group

    4 minutes—Comment on their feelings and tell about the purpose of the group and how the group is going to be conducted. Confidentiality If possible, let me know if they are going to miss or be late Tell about cutting off and that I'll be looking around and not always looking at the person who is talking

Middle Phase

2 minutes—Word or phrase round of what is the hardest thing
for them right now regarding their recovery. (See
page 174 for a discussion of rounds.)

30 minutes—Discuss their comments
Probable topics:
Having extra time on their hands
Missing old friends
Having emotions for the first time
Believing that they can control drink

5 minutes—Dyads (pairs)—what stood out to them about the
discussion

5 minutes—Process dyads (hear comments and reactions)

10 minutes—1-10 round regarding comfort in the group and then
talk about how the group can be helpful

20 minutes—Focus on one or two members' specific issues
[Back-up plan—talk about self-talk and RET or
the importance of working a recovery program]

Closing Phase

5 minutes—Dyads (pairs)—talk about what stood out to them
about the session

10 minutes—Get comments, summarize, use closing round on
what stood out

This leader carefully planned each phase of the session and understood that it was the beginning stage since it was the first session. The leader planned to discuss the purpose of the group, the ground rules, and her leadership style. She planned to mention how at times she may need to cut off some discussions and that she would be looking around when someone was talking in order to see other members' reactions. She planned to use dyads a couple of times so that members could get a chance to get to know two members better by talking in pairs. For the middle phase, she planned to focus on the members' comments regarding what has been hardest about recovery. She gave thought to the probable topics and planned to either focus on a couple of members, teach the idea of how one's self-talk causes one's feelings, or discuss the importance of working a recovery program. Since it was to be the first session, she planned a discussion about the comfort level in the group, and she specifically thought out how she was going to close the group.

Following is another leader's plan for the third session of an incest survivors' group.

<u>Warm-up Phase</u>

    10 minutes—Thoughts from the last session or thoughts from the week

<u>Middle Phase</u>

    3 minutes—Introduce topic of shame—how it is different from guilt

    5 minutes—Comment round hearing how shame fits into their thinking

    30 minutes—Discuss their comments
        Possible topics:
            Blaming self
            Thinking they are bad because they didn't stop it
            Being told they were bad
            Feeling bad about their behavior since then

    40 minutes—Focus on one or two members regarding shame [Back-up plan: Use two chairs—one small chair and one large chair with the word "Now" on it to represent the present. Have them each talk about shame then and whether they need to feel shame now.]

<u>Closing Phase</u>

    7 minutes—Dyads as to what stood out

    10 minutes—Closing, sharing, wishes for each other

The leader allowed time at the beginning for comments and sharing and then planned to go into a discussion of shame by first giving a brief description of shame as it relates to incest and then using a comment round to focus the members. He planned to funnel the topic of shame by making sure that meaningful dialogue took place. He also planned to work with one or two members on shame. As a back-up plan he would use chairs to help members see that they do not have to feel shame now. The leader allowed quite a bit of time for closing since the topic of shame is such an important one for incest survivors.

I cannot emphasize enough the importance of planning, and yet so many participants at my group workshops comment that they either do not plan or plan very superficially. Planning almost insures that the group will be productive and beneficial.

FOCUS

The impact therapist understands that the most important task of a group leader is to focus the group. The Impact therapist knows that in order for a group to be meaningful, members have to focus. Therefore, he is always thinking about what to focus on. He listens for or initiates topics that are relevant to the purpose of the group. He also focuses on one person when it is seems that spending time helping that member would be valuable for the member and relevant for the other members. The following examples show how the impact therapist focuses the session.

Example 1

Judith: I never ever thought it would be this hard. Alzheimer's disease is horrible.

Jake: Sometimes I want to scream. It is so hard to watch her mind slowly deteriorate. I keep doing more and more for her, but nothing helps. Every now and then I get mad and yell at her, and she cries; then I feel guilty.

Ellen: Yesterday, I went to get Mom from the porch, and she had wandered off down the street. I'm so glad she didn't get into the street. It's so hard having to watch her almost every second.

Leader: Let's focus for a few minutes on the frustrations that all of you are feeling and how to deal with them. Then we can focus on guilt feelings that some of you have. Both topics are good ones, and I think a good discussion can help each of you. I want you to think of what is the most frustrating or hardest thing for you about this disease.

The leader heard different topics and focused the group on one of them: frustration. He also cued the group to the next topic: guilt. He decided at this time not to focus on Jake, but rather on the topic. He made a mental note to possibly go back to Jake, especially when the group discusses guilt.

Example 2

Louie: When my daddy is drunk, he fights with my mommy. I try to stop him. Sometimes he gets real mad at me.

Woody: I never know what to do when Ralph is drunk. I hide under my bed most of the time. Sometimes it gets so bad, I sneak out and go to my grandma's. I always feel bad if I leave because I worry about what will happen to Mom.

Leader:	That's a good topic for all of us to talk about. What is the most important thing to remember when your parent is drunk?
Jamie:	To be real quiet.
Leader:	That's a good idea. It may not be the most important thing. Somebody else want to make a stab at what is the most important thing to remember.
Bill:	To make sure you are safe?
Leader:	That's right! Always make sure you are safe. Let's talk about how to make sure you are safe.

The leader knows that a very important topic for children of alcoholics is safety when a parent is drunk. The leader focused the members on the topic by asking the question about safety and then initiated a discussion about how to be safe.

Example 3

Sara:	(*Tearing*) I am discriminated against because I am short. I hate going out because of the way people look at me.
Liz:	That's terrible that people do that. People are so insensitive. My mother-in-law is like that. The other day when I was over, she started telling me about…
Leader:	(*Knowing that Liz has a tendency to talk on and on*) Liz, I want us to get back to Sara. (*Looks at Sara*) Would you like to talk about how that feels and get some help?
Sara:	I don't know what anyone can do to help.
Leader:	I think we can help. Say some more about how you feel.

In this example, the leader saw the need to cut off Liz and focus on Sara since she was in pain, and the purpose of the group was to help members feel better about themselves.

Example 4

Nate:	Last week I got so mad when Joey came in and took that stuff from my locker.
Robert:	Yeah, something has got to be done about Joey. He drives me crazy. Something is the matter with him. I'm going to really punch him out. I know I'll get in trouble, but I can't help it. I'm just waiting for the right time.
Paula:	I'm glad you are going to get him. What about Billy Bob? He's just as bad.

Leader: Robert, let's talk about your anger for a minute. (*Holds up short piece of string*) See this? (*Everyone looks at the string.*) This is your fuse when it comes to Joey. I think what we need to do for you, and for most of you, is to lengthen your fuse. (*Holds up a longer fuse*) I don't think you really want to get in trouble and lose privileges. Do you?

Robert: He's a jerk. Somebody has to teach him a lesson!

Leader: Do you want to lose privileges?

Robert: (*Pauses; in a thinking voice*) You're right. But what do I do?

Leader: We can talk about that here. There's lots we can do.

The leader saw the need to focus the session on Robert and did not let the topic go to a discussion about Billy Bob. The impact therapist always thinks about how to focus the group so it is productive and, in this case, felt that the session was not going to focus on anything meaningful unless she intervened.

In these four examples, the impact therapist focused on a topic or person as the need arose in the group. Zeroing in on a person or topic as it emerges from the content is one of the major ways in which the impact therapist focuses the group.

Additional Techniques for Focusing

Handouts

A handout may be information, a story, or a sentence completion activity. Good handouts focus members because they provide members with something to respond to.

Making a list on the chalkboard or flip chart

Members very often stay focused when the group is generating a list that is being written down for all to see. The list can be of many different things such as possible choices, characteristics of a good spouse, ways to have fun without spending much money, or things to do in the evening after work.

Exercises

Using group exercises is a very good way to focus the members on a specific topic. The impact therapist understands the importance of picking the right exercise from the many different kinds, which include writing, movement, dyads and triads, rounds, arts and crafts, fantasy, common readings, feedback, trust, experiential, moral dilemmas, and group decision making. In *Group Counseling: Strategies and Skills* (Jacobs et al., 1994), I describe in considerable detail the kinds of exercises, how to choose the right exercise, and how to introduce and conduct an exercise. Here I discuss some exercises that are good specifically for focusing the group.

Having members form dyads and talk about a subject can be an excellent way to focus the members on a topic. Having members give each other feedback by using one of the many different feedback exercises certainly gets the members focused on themselves and other group members. Doing a drawing or a project out of clay regarding some aspect of their lives usually works to focus members. Having members move to different spots in the room or along a continuum regarding a particular issue focuses members because they have to think about where to position themselves. Written activities also can quickly focus the members on a topic. Family sculpture or group sculpture can be a very thought-provoking and powerful exercise to focus members on their families or on the group.

Rounds

I use rounds more than any other technique to focus the group because they are quick and simple, involve everyone, and can be quite thought provoking. Rounds also encourage participation. There are three different kinds of rounds: the designated word or number round; the word or phrase round; and the comment round.

The designated word or number round is a round where the members can only say certain words, such as "Yes/No" or "Here/Getting Here/Not Here," or some number on a scale. Both of these rounds can be helpful during the warm-up phase to get an idea of what the members are thinking and if they are ready to begin group.

Example 1

Leader:	Let's start. First, I'd like to do a simple round of "Here/Getting Here/Not Here" regarding how you are feeling about your readiness to start group today. Say "here" if you are ready, "not here" if you are not, or "getting here" if you are sort of here. This is a good way for me to get a sense of how each of you are feeling. Who wants to go first?
Ruth:	Here.
Andrea:	Getting here.
Carol:	Here.
Jan:	Not here.
Lee:	Getting here.
Leader:	Is there anything we can do to help those of you who are not here to get here?
Jan:	I don't feel good physically. I'll just have to see how it goes. I may need to leave.
Leader:	I'm glad you told us. Sure hope you feel better.
Andrea:	I'll get here. I've had a tough week. I may want to get some input from the group regarding what I should do.

The leader gained much information about the members by doing the round. Also the round tends to get members focused on starting the group. The "Yes/No" round can be similar except the leader is trying to find out if members have something they want to work on or if they want to discuss some issue.

Example 2

Leader:	(*Seeing that the warm-up phase is winding down*) Let's do a quick check of who wants time today in group. We'll do a "Yes/No" round with "yes" being you do have something you want to bring up today.
Mark:	No.
Randy:	No.

Kyle:	Yes.
Dale:	Yes.
Kenny:	No.
Leader:	Briefly, Kyle, what is your yes about?
Kyle:	I want to talk about seeing my ex-wife out on a date last Friday.
Dale:	I want to talk about getting through this Saturday which would be my sixth anniversary.

By doing this round, the leader focused the members and very quickly learned which members wanted to talk and what they wanted to talk about.

Example 3

The "Yes/No" round can also be used to get a quick assessment if members want to do something.

Leader:	Let's do a "Yes/No" round regarding talking about the guilt. "Yes" if you think it would be a good topic and "no" if you don't.
Lana:	No.
Ellen:	Yes, most definitely!
Michelle:	Yes.
Manuel:	Yes. It's a good topic!
Hero:	Yes.
Tammy:	No.
Keleigh:	Yes.

Given that most said "yes," the leader would focus on guilt since it is a very important emotion to understand, it fits with the purpose of the group, and the leader has given some thought of how to introduce and work the topic of guilt in this group.

The 1-10 round is an excellent tool for getting members focused and getting information quickly. I have had members rate such things as their week, job, parents, in-laws, love relationship, sex life, stress, and parenting ability. I have also had members rate how much they feel guilt, anger, fear, worry, jealousy, and self-love on a 1-10 scale. The follow-up question of "What is between your rating and a 10?" helps focus on the idea of change. The examples below show how a leader can use the designated number round.

Example 4

Leader: I want us to spend some time on how to make work better for you. To get a sense of how you feel about your job, I want you to rate it on a 1-10, with 10 being "great" and 1 being "hate it."

Jimmy: 7.

Richard: 5.

Al: 6.

Sharon: 3.

Mike: 8.

Leader: I want you to think about why you picked the number you picked and also what could raise your number one or two points. (*Pause*) Comments?

Richard: I like my job okay, but I am bored. What would raise my rating would be some new challenges.

Example 5

Leader: We seem to be sort of bouncing from topic to topic. I'd like to zero in on your communication with your lover. On a 1-10 scale, with 10 being "we communicate great" and 1 being "we don't communicate," how would you rate your current communication with your partner?

Jackie: It's about a 4 now. It used to be a 10. I don't know what happened.

Rose: About a 6.

Sandy: 9.

Charity: 3.

Lisa: 5.

Leader: This looks like an area that we can work on. Especially your part in the communication. Sandy, at some point, we'll get you to share why yours is going so well. Let me ask this as a follow up: Are your ratings better or worse than they would have been a year ago?

Example 6

Leader: Since this is the first meeting and we've been here for about an hour, I'd like to do a round regarding each person's comfort in the group. We'll put this on a 1-10 scale, with 10 being very comfortable and 1 being very uncomfortable. I'd like you to do two numbers, the first one being your comfort level right when we started and the second one being your comfort level now.

Marcia: 2 when we started; 8 now.

Fran: 4 when we started; 9 now.

Dottie: 1 when we started; about a 5 now.

Martina: 3 and now 9.

Lorrie: 2 and now 5 or 6.

Tanya: 3 and 7.

Leader: What has helped you get more comfortable, and what else could we do that might help?

In each of these rounds, the leader focused the group on some topic and had members do a 1-10 rating and then followed up with a question that kept the group focused on the topic.

The word or phrase round gives members a chance to comment with just a couple of words regarding some topic. The benefit of the word or phrase round is that it is quick, and everyone gets a chance to talk. It is used when the leader wants everyone to give a very brief comment.

Example

Leader: We're going to get away from things at school and talk for a few minutes about life at home. Just to get a sense of how things go at home, I want each of you to think of a word or phrase that describes your home life. Your word could be anything such as loving, war, sports, business, chaotic, distant, close, alone, fighting, alcohol, religion, or busy. Think of any word or phrase that you think captures the tone in your house.

Troy: I'll start. Sad. My mom is so sad about the divorce, and that was 2 years ago. Dad is…

Leader: (*Holds hand out, signaling Troy to stop; using a warm voice*) Troy, let's just do a word now, and then we'll come back for comments.

Mel: Loving but busy.

Dave: Chaotic.

Candy: Caring from Mom, distant from Dad.

Toby: Sports.

Mitch: Alcohol and fighting.

Leader: Let's talk about how you feel about what you said. How would you like things to be different?

The round got members focused, and then the leader started in on a discussion about home life. The round also very quickly provided some good information for the leader which he could use to get group members to talk more about their lives at home.

The comment round is similar to the word or phrase round except it allows each member more time to comment. The leader uses a comment round to hear from everyone and to keep the more dominate members from monopolizing.

Example

Leader: (*Having just completed some intense work with Phil regarding his anger at his dad*) I want to get a sense of what each of you is thinking, having watched Phil do what he did. Briefly, what did Phil's work mean to you or cause you to think about? Don't focus on Phil, but rather focus on yourself.

Chuck: I don't know if I could do what Phil did. I would like to talk about my situation, but I am afraid that I'll cry.

Leader: (*Very warm voice*) And that would be okay. We'll come back to you if you'd like.

Chuck: I think so.

Jim: I was thinking that I need to write my dad a letter just to get stuff off my chest. From watching Phil, I realized how mad I am at him for leaving, and I need to say it to him somehow.

Diana: I'm okay with my dad, but not with Mom. What Phil was doing could have been me and my mom. I'd like to work on that if we have time.

Cliff: I am still very afraid of my parents. I saw what they did to my sister, and that was horrible. They threw her out because she kissed this black guy. They are very narrow minded!! I live in constant fear.

Leader: Phil, I think you did some good work and obviously triggered work for others. We still have about 25 minutes. Who wants to work?

Diana: I do if no one else does.

The leader knew that Phil's work had generated much energy in the members; and by using the round to focus members on themselves, she got a sense of what each member was thinking. If she had not used the round, a member, such as Diana, could have started sharing, and the others would not have gotten to share their feelings. She then focused the group on Diana by simply asking who wanted to work.

The impact therapist uses the round frequently when leading groups because this technique is very useful for focusing the group, gathering information, and getting members involved.

Creative techniques

Creative techniques are very useful in groups since they tend to cause members to focus. These techniques can be divided into five categories: props, chairs, movement, writings and drawings, and fantasies (Jacobs, 1992). In my previous books on group counseling (1994) and creative counseling (1992), I discussed fully how these techniques can be used in group settings. Here I briefly discuss some creative techniques and give examples that show how those creative techniques can be used to focus the session. In the next section on funneling, I continue some of the examples to illustrate how, once the members are focused, the leader funnels the group below 7 using the members' comments and the creative technique.

Props. Many different props, such as cups, shields, filters, fuses, tapes, and blocks, can be used to focus the group.

<u>Cups</u>. The leader can hold up a cup and discuss how it can represent one's self-esteem and how each person has leaks in his or her self-esteem.

Example

Leader: I want each of you to think of this cup as your self-esteem. (*Everyone is staring at the leader who has a cup in her hand.*) If the cup has no holes, then it will stay full if we pour something into it; but if it has holes, then it will leak. From what you have said, each of you has different leaks in your self-esteem. (*Takes pencil and punches three holes*) I want you to think about what your leaks are about. They could be about your appearance, your past, your abilities, or whatever. The important thing is that you identify what your leaks in your self-esteem are.

This technique works even better when the leader gives each member his or her own cup to punch holes in.

<u>Shields</u>. Helping members understand that they can shield themselves from others by thinking and deflecting hostile comments is often an important concept that arises in certain groups.

Example

Leader: A number of you have been talking about hurtful people in your lives, and I want to show you a way to protect yourself. (*Holding up a 12 x 12 piece of Plexiglass*) This represents a shield that all of you need. If you have a shield, when people say mean things, you can hold up your shield and deflect the comment rather than letting it in because, if you let it in, it hurts. Bill, come up here and poke me in the shoulder. (*Leader demonstrates letting himself be poked and then demonstrates shielding himself to deflect the poke.*)

Filters. The filter works differently than the shield in that the filter can be used as symbolic of letting in the good but blocking out the bad.

Example

Leader: I think it would be helpful for all of you to consider using a filter with those two teachers. (*Holds up a furnace filter*) All of you agree that they are not all bad and that they are good at teaching the subjects they teach. It is their other comments that are hard to take, so a filter seems like it would help. Why do you think I am asking you to use a filter?

Tom: Because filters take the dirt and crap out.

Leader: What about the good stuff?

Sid: It gets through. I guess what you are saying is that we should filter the comments but let the teaching come through. That's hard to do.

Leader: I know it is, and that's why filters exist. If you don't use a filter, you're not going to learn anything; plus you probably will get in trouble because you'll take on the teacher. What do others of you think about this filter idea?

Tapes. Cassette tapes can be used in many effective ways since counseling can often be seen as replacing or editing tapes that are in the client's head. In the example below, the leader talks about making a new tape.

Example

Leader: I want each of you to realize something. When you were growing up, you made a tape about yourself; and now you play that tape in your head. (*Holds up a cassette tape to her ear as if she is listening to it*) I want you to think about what is on your tape. I think most of you have lots of negative things on your tape due to your home life and other experiences that you had early in life. One purpose of this group is to help you feel better, and in order to do that, you need to make new tapes. (*Leader gives each member a brand new tape that is still wrapped.*) I'd like you to think if you would like to make a new tape.

Blocks. Showing how things don't fit, nearly fit, or fit can be very helpful. Blocks can be used to show the fit of friendships, relationships, families, jobs, and many other situations where there is a fit of some sort. In the following example, the leader is working with a couples' group and quickly focuses the members on the fit of their relationships.

Example

Leader: I want you to look at these blocks and this peg and think about which configuration would symbolize your relationship. (*Leader has three blocks with different size holes and a peg that is obviously too big for one, nearly fits another and fits one.*) Is your relationship the near fit, the good fit, or the impossible fit. (*All stare at the blocks.*)

Chairs. There are many different ways that chairs can be used to focus members on an idea or topic. Chairs can be used as a group exercise as in the first example or as part of a member's work, as in the second example. By using a chair or chairs as part of someone's work, the leader not only focuses the working member but also the other members since they can mentally put themselves in the two chairs.

Example 1

Leader: (*Having decided to focus on the topic of anger, puts a chair in the center of group*) I want each of you to think of someone you are currently or were recently angry with. Put that person in this seat. (*Everyone stares at the chair.*) I'm going to ask each of you to tell who that person is in your life, such as lover, spouse, mother, boss, brother, or whoever.

Example 2

Leader: (*Placing two chairs, about 8 feet apart, in the middle of the group*) Suzy, let me show you what you are doing. It's like you are going back and forth between these two seats. When you get in one seat, you start thinking about the other. I want you to come sit in one seat, then move to the other. Do this about five or six times. (*Suzy does this while others watch.*)

Suzy: This is what I do all the time in my mind.

Leader: I know, and you don't get much done except to expend a lot of energy. Can any of you relate to this?

Doris: I was thinking about my decision to switch jobs. Suzy, I'm doing exactly what you are doing!

Leon: I just realized the game I play with myself. It's like I strap myself into one seat for a while, and then I slowly unstrap myself and go to the other seat and then start the process all over again. I think that I'm making progress, but seeing this makes me realize that I'm not.

Example 3

Leader: It's become clear to me that all of you have a tendency to put people above you. (*Pulling up a chair and standing on it*) I want you to think of the people you have in this chair whom you put above you and whom you are afraid of. (*Everyone looks up and thinks.*) I'll do a quick round of some of the main people you have above you, and then we'll talk about what can be done to get them off the chair. (*Leader sits back down.*)

Example 4

Leader: I want each of you to look at these two chairs. Note one is labeled "THEN," and one is labeled "NOW." As you go about living your life, how much do you let the pain, memories, or behaviors from your past affect your life in the present? In other words, do you live your life from the NOW seat or the THEN seat? (*All stare at the two chairs.*)

Shelly: I live mine mostly in the THEN seat. I am always thinking about the past and how I have screwed up in so many ways.

Mark: I can get in the NOW seat when I go to sporting events, but other than that, my mind is usually back in the past or in the future.

Leader: That's a good point. (*Pulls up a third chair and writes "LATER" on a piece of paper and tapes it to the chair*) Some of you may live in the future and past, but not the present.

Example 5

Leader: (*Puts small chair in the center*) I want each of you to think how your little girl or little boy gets in the way or acts out during the holidays. (*Everyone stares at the chair.*)

Otis: I still go home wanting my parents to be different. They favor my sister, and I feel hurt and usually get in a fight with one of them just to get some attention.

Amy: I feel bad because I'm not married, and all my brothers and sisters are. I think they all talk about what is wrong with me. I hate it when they ask about my social life!

Jim: I'm not married, and I don't have any family that I visit. I just feel real sorry for myself.

Toni: I'm hurt when I don't get cards from people even though I haven't sent cards for 2 years now. I also spend a lot of time worrying about buying the exact right gift for everyone.

In each of these examples, the chair or chairs definitely helped to make a concept more concrete and provided an object for members to look at, keeping them focused on whatever the object represented.

Movement. The impact therapist always considers whether the members may benefit from moving or seeing some members move. The use of movement is a good way to focus members because it is experiential in that the members have to do something. In some of the examples above, the members moved from chair to chair, or the leader or someone stood in a chair. These movement activities usually cause members to focus on whatever the movement is concerning. Family sculpture is a very focused and engaging movement exercise where a member positions other members, who represent his family members, into a pose. Group sculpture is a movement exercise where members position themselves according to how they feel about the group (Jacobs, 1992). Another exercise, which I use quite frequently, is the values continuum where members have to decide where they are on the continuum, as in the example below.

Example

Leader: I want you to stand up, come to the center of the room, and line up behind one another. (*Members do this.*) I'm going to have you position yourselves along a continuum, with the wall on my left being "working hard to change" and the wall on my right being "not working to change." When I count to three, I want you to place yourselves somewhere between the two walls. One (*pause*), two (*pause*), three. (*Everyone moves.*)

This exercise gets members focused on how hard they are working in the group. Value lines can also be conducted regarding many different topics, such as how finished or unfinished one is with the past, parents, or former lovers; how satisfied one is with her life, marriage or job; or how much guilt, anger, or jealousy one feels. I know of many group leaders that start the middle phase of each session with a values continuum as a way to focus the group.

These are just some of the many different ways to use movement to focus a group. I always keep the idea of movement in my mind because not only is it good for focusing, but it also helps energize members if they are tired. The moving around helps members get reengaged if they have begun to drift off.

Writings and Drawings. The impact therapist is always thinking about making the group interesting, productive, and focused. Having members write or draw something is a very effective way to get them focused on an issue. Having them list characteristics about themselves, their families, their friends, or their coworkers quickly gets members focused. I sometimes have members write for a couple of minutes on a topic such as self-worth, anger, love, need for approval, or fear of failure. Having members draw their houses or their families focuses them and opens the door to many different discussions. Using TA, I often have group members draw their ego states or an egogram (see chapter 2). Getting members to graph their lives on a 1-10 scale for the last 5 or 10 years and for the next few years is an excellent way to focus on the past, present, and future.

Fantasies. A very effective technique for focusing members is the use of fantasy. For instance, having members imagine that they are an animal, a car, or a tree can get members into the fantasy and then into different topics as each discusses his or her fantasy. One very simple fantasy that I use quite often is the common object fantasy where I point to an object, such as a briefcase or a flip chart, and have members fantasize that they are that object and what their lives would be like as that object. Other fantasies that I use frequently are having members imagine that they are in a hot air balloon, and there are weights that are keeping them from taking off; or they are at the movie theater, and the movie is about their lives. I ask them to look at the credits for the director, producer, and the main characters. Then I have them imagine watching the movie and then, when leaving the theater, listening to others comment about the movie.

Focusing the group is the key for impact. By using many different kinds of focusing techniques, the impact therapist keeps the group interested, energized, and focused. Once the session is focused, the impact therapist funnels the session for further impact.

FUNNEL

In chapter 7, I discussed in great detail the importance of funneling a session with one client. The same is true for group sessions. **Most impact occurs when the leader funnels the session.** Funneling group sessions is much more difficult because there are more people bringing up more topics, and members try to steer the group in many different directions. The key to an effective group is funneling below **7** on topics and issues that are relevant to the purpose of the group. The impact therapist thinks about the purpose and then tries to focus the group on a relevant issue or person. Once the group is focused, the leader tries to funnel the session to a meaningful level by using good leadership skills that engage and involve the members and by using theory and creative techniques.

The leader always considers whether the session needs to funnel. Most funneling takes place during the middle phase, but the impact therapist may take a few minutes during the warmup or even the closing to funnel on some concept or person. There are times when something comes up where a brief in-depth discussion can be helpful even though it is during the opening or closing of the session. During the middle phase, the leader is always thinking about the depth of the group and tries to funnel the group if it is not going below **7**. The leader will funnel discussion of relevant topics or funnel by focusing on a person who needs and wants to work on some issue. In observing leaders who use the facilitator model, I notice that they often wait too long to funnel the session or wait for the members to funnel, which often does not happen. The impact therapist knows it is her responsibility to funnel the session.

How To Funnel a Session

When the impact therapist decides to funnel a session, she will often use a lower, slower voice which signals the members to try to go to a deeper level. She will also use the variety of skills and techniques which are discussed in the following sections.

Cut off "surface type stories"

Even when the group is focused on a person or topic, members often will keep the session from funneling by exchanging stories that have little meaning or letting one member become long winded. To funnel the session, the leader has to cut off these stories in order to allow other members who may want to share at a deeper level the opportunity to do so. It is the leader's responsibility to prevent members from taking up valuable time with irrelevant or even relevant stories, especially when it is apparent that the members can go to a deeper level. Certainly members' sharing is valuable, but letting members go on and on is not helpful for anyone and prevents funneling. One of the major reasons why groups do not funnel to a meaningful level is due to the leader's letting members tell stories that get triggered by other members' comments.

Ask a good, thought-provoking question (not a "story" question)

Once the session is focused on either a topic or person, a good question can cause members to think or feel more about an issue. This, in turn, creates a greater chance that the discussion will funnel to a meaningful level. What often happens is a leader gets the group focused, but he does not ask questions that tend to funnel the session. Listed below are a few examples of some thought-provoking, funneling questions that would be asked in a slow, deliberate tone of voice. These questions tend to get members to think.

- What do you want to do differently?
- What are you doing that does not work?
- What do you need to do to finish your unfinished business?
- What part do you think you play in your marital problems?
- What do you think you could do to improve your grades?
- How do you seek approval at your job, and how does that feel?
- How long does one have to feel bad about what happened to him or her as a child?

Each of these questions would have a tendency to get members to explore their thoughts and/or feelings and, thus, funnel the group to a deeper level.

Very consciously hold the focus on either a topic or a person

One way the impact therapist gets a session to funnel is to not let the members go from topic to topic or person to person once the session is focused. For example, if the session is focused on job dissatisfaction and then the members keep talking about all kinds of dissatisfaction rather one specific kind, such as working conditions, the session will not funnel. Or if one person starts to talk about his dissatisfaction, another member's jumping in would prevent funneling. By consciously keeping the group focused on one topic or one person and getting members to share at a more personal level, the leader will funnel the session to *6* or below.

Example 1

Rick: At work, I feel very much an outsider and feel that I am always trying to get people to notice and appreciate me.

Fran: I never feel that I deserve the job that I have. I started out in the warehouse, and now I am in management. I just never feel comfortable when I am in my office. I can't believe that it is me who has an office!

Boyd: They just painted my office. I now have to order new furniture, and I've been looking through all these catalogs.

Fran: I'd be glad to help you. I did my office just a few weeks ago. My next project is picking out wallpaper. I'd like to get the group's help on some colors. I'm not too good at picking colors.

Leader: Let's do that if we have time, or perhaps you can get some ideas after the group. But let's stay with the topic of how you feel in relationship to your work or the feelings you have at work. There seems to be a variety of feelings that many of you have, and I think we can have a good session sharing and talking about those feelings.

Leonard: I worry all the time about pleasing everyone at work. I never feel totally relaxed because I'm so worried someone won't like what I am doing.

Belinda: Ever since I became shift manager, I've been uncomfortable. There are 10 people working under me who are old enough to be my parents. Two are nearly old enough to be my grandparents. It's very uncomfortable.

Fran: Come to think of it, I have some of those same feelings. I didn't realize that until you just mentioned it. How do we get over the feeling of being too young to be a manager.

Leonard: Do either of you sense that the people resent your being in the position?

Belinda: I don't really. In fact, everyone seems pleased that I am the shift manager.

Leonard: So you're saying the problem is in your head?

Belinda: I've never thought of it, but that's right.

Example 2

Caroline: I have trouble sleeping at night. I know it's strange to say, and I've never told anyone this, but I fear that I won't wake up in the morning.

Cindy: I don't sleep well either. I often get up at 2:00 and stay up until 5:00 and then go back to sleep.

Sherry: What do you do between 2:00 and 5:00?

Leader:	Wait. Let's go back to Caroline. Would you like to talk about that some more?
Caroline:	Yes, I think I would.
Leader:	Why don't you tell us more about your thoughts about not waking up and the fears you have about that.
Caroline:	As it gets close to bedtime, I start thinking, "Could this be my last night on earth? Will I wake up and get to see my kids off to school, or will they find me dead?"

In both of these examples, the leader did not let the focus shift to another topic since he knows that groups tend not to funnel when the focus keeps changing. In the first example, the leader held the focus on the topic of feelings and did not let it shift to decorating the office. In the second example, the leader saw that he could funnel the session by focusing on Caroline, who was obviously in pain.

Use a thought-provoking round, exercise, or creative technique that gets everyone thinking and then funnel the members' comments or feelings

Some rounds and exercises can be very thought provoking or elicit much emotion. The skill of the leader comes in getting those thoughts and feelings expressed so that the group funnels to a deeper level. Some leaders make the mistake of letting members make very surface comments or focusing on one member when several members have much to say and share. I have seen many leaders conduct excellent exercises but then not funnel the members' reactions. **The key to any exercise is the meaningful sharing as a result of the exercise.** In the examples below, the impact therapist makes sure that the discussion after the round or exercise funnels to a deeper level.

Example 1

Leader:	(*Having completed a 1-10 round regarding how members feel about their stepparents*) Many of you gave very low numbers. Briefly, I'd like to hear why you rated your relationship so low, and then we'll discuss ways to change it, if possible.
Roy:	I don't like it when he tries to tell me what to do. He's not my dad!
Morris:	It's my stepmom. She doesn't do things the way Mom did, and she has all these weird rules about keeping things perfectly neat. Mom never was like that.

Polly: My stepdad is loud, and he hogs the television. He makes me watch all sports shows, and I don't get to watch anything I like.

Kathleen: My stepdad is mean to my dog. He won't let her in the house.

Leader: That gives me some idea of what is happening between you and your stepparent. Would all of you agree that you would like your life to be better at home? (*All nod except Roy.*) Roy, you look hesitant.

Roy: Me and my stepdad get in fights all the time. Mom says I cause them. Maybe I do! I wish Mom would never have married him! I keep thinking that she might divorce him and take Dad back. Dad sure wants Mom back. He tells me that all the time.

Leader: Roy, I think we can help you, but first I'd like to hear how the rest of you feel about your parents getting back together, except for you, Morris, since your mom is no longer living.

Kathleen: I used to think about it, but I've pretty much accepted that it's not going to happen. My parents are friends, but they just don't love each other enough to be married to each other.

Polly: I wish my parents were friends. They fight all the time. They are better off being divorced.

Leader: So that's not an issue for the rest of you. Let's see if we can help Roy then. I would guess you get in fights because you think if your mom and your stepdad divorce, then maybe she'll get back with your dad.

Roy: (*Head hanging down*) I think you're right. I haven't been nice at all, and the guy is not really a bad guy. Mom really likes him.

Leader: If they did get divorced, do you really believe that your mom would go back to your dad?

Roy: (*Pause, in a sad voice*) I want to believe it, but Mom says she would never go back to him because of his drinking. She doesn't let me see him too much because of the drinking. She probably would find another man rather than go back with Dad.

Leader:	Roy, I want you to think about that for a few minutes, and then we'll come back to you. Think about what you can do differently. Others of you, what can you do differently.
Kathleen:	I could try to be nice and keep my dog real clean; then he may let her in. I could promise only to have her in my room.
Leader:	Those are good ideas. Have you talked to your mom about this?
Kathleen:	No, not really. We had a couple of fights about it.
Leader:	What do others of you think about Kathleen's ideas?
Polly:	I have found that being nice sometimes works better than fighting. I think I need to try to ask in a nicer way about sharing the television; or maybe if I am real nice, they would get me a television for my room.
Leader:	Talking is better than fighting. (*Pulls up two chairs—one is small*) If you are in this chair (*the big chair*), you try to make things better and talk with your parents and step-parent; and if you are in this chair (*the little chair*), you fight with them. Which chair do you sit in the most? (*All point to the little chair.*) How would you act if you sat in the big chair instead of the little chair? Kathleen has said what she might do. How about others?
Polly:	I think I need to sit in the big chair.
Roy:	I could quit trying to break them up.
Leader:	What do you think of Roy's idea about not trying to break them up?
Morris:	That seems like a good idea since you said your mom and dad would not get back together anyway. I've just been thinking that my dad is happy because...
Leader:	Let's finish this with Roy, and then we'll come to your thoughts about your dad.
Roy:	I think this has helped me. I guess I have to realize that they are not going to get back together.
Leader:	What about sharing this with your mom? I bet she would be glad to hear this.
Roy:	I think I will!
Leader:	Morris, what were you saying?

Morris: I've just been thinking that my dad is happy that he met Gloria, and I think I can at least be happy for him. Gloria is okay, but she's not my mom. That's not her fault. I think I have been mad at her because she took Mom's place, but Mom can't be here because she died.

Leader: I am real impressed how all of you are coming up with ideas from the big chair.

In this example, the leader used the round to focus the group and then funneled the session by getting them to express their thoughts and feelings. The leader stayed with the theme of what they could do to get along better with their stepparents. The leader heard from everyone to see if they had similar issues instead of immediately focusing on Roy. The leader funneled the discussion to **5** by staying with the theme and asking what they could do differently and by using the two chairs to help them see they had a choice in how they responded. All the members seemed to be thinking about new ideas regarding getting along better.

Example 2

Leader: We're going to get away from things at school and talk for a few minutes about life at home. Just to get a sense of how things go at home, I want each of you to think of a word or phase that describes your home life. Your word could be anything, such as loving, war, sports, business, chaotic, distant, close, alone, fighting, alcohol, religion, or busy. Think of any word or phase that you think captures the tone in your house.

Troy: I'll start. Sad. My mom is so sad about the divorce, and that was 2 years ago. Dad is...

Leader: (*Holds hand out, signaling Troy to stop; using a warm voice*) Troy, let's just do a word now, and then we'll come back for comments.

Mel: Loving but busy.

Candy: Caring from Mom, distant from Dad.

Toby: Sports.

Mitch: Alcohol and fighting.

Leader: Let's talk about how you feel about what you said. Do you wish it were different, and if so, how would you like things to be different?

Candy: My mom is nice, but it is my dad who is distant. He never shows any caring. Sometimes I think he doesn't care. He has never once come to one of my sporting events, but he has gone to all of my brother's.

Toby: Heck, I wish my dad didn't come to my games. He's on me all the time about how I am doing. The few times he was not there I felt much more relaxed. I don't even know if I am going to play next year. The pressure from Dad is getting to me, but I don't know how I could tell him that I want to quit. Actually, I don't want to quit; I just want him to quit trying to live through me.

Troy: I don't know how to help Mom. She is so lonely; I feel guilty if I go out with the guys or a date on the weekends, so I mostly stay at home.

Toby: I didn't know that. I knew you always said no when we asked you to go to the movies or something, but I never knew why.

Troy: (*Tearing up*) What am I to do? She cries and asks me to stay home and watch a movie with her.

Leader: (*Using a very warm, nurturing voice*) There's a lot going on here, and I think we can help each other. Let me hear from the others, and then we'll come back and work on as many of these issues as we can today and then do the rest next meeting.

Mitch: I hate being at my house, with all the fighting and drinking. I am always thinking about protecting my mom, and a couple of times I have gotten my baseball bat and told Dad to get out.

Mel: That's horrible. I can't even imagine that. I saw a movie once that...

Leader: (*Cutting off to keep the session below 7*) Let's stay with Mitch for a minute. (*Using a warm, nurturing voice*) Mitch, have you ever talked to anyone about this?

Mitch: No, I have been too ashamed. I started to lie in group today, but it's bad.

Leader: I'm glad you shared. I'm glad all of you shared. Now let's try to help each other feel better about their home life. Mel, you seemed to be okay about your home life. Is that right?

Mel: Yes, everyone is very busy, but it is not bad.

Leader: Good. I'm sure you'll have some helpful things to say. Mitch, why don't we start with you. Tell us some more.

The leader saw that this session could be very helpful to all the members except for perhaps Mel. She got everyone to share, and their comments seemed to indicate that most members were below **7** and needed to go even deeper. The leader cut off Mel when he was going to shift to the movie he saw because she wanted to keep the session funneled at the level it was; also, she knew that Mitch needed support and further work. She decided to briefly get Mel to comment, and then she moved to Mitch but was ready to move to other members if Mitch seemed uncomfortable. She also decided to funnel the session on a person rather than a topic since each person had different concerns about his or her home life. She was confident the session would stay at a deep level because Mitch already was at **5**. She knew if she did not waste time, she could work with Mitch and also work with Troy and possibly one other person before the session ended.

In the next example, the impact therapist uses a creative technique to get members to funnel to **6**, and then he makes sure that the discussion stays funneled.

Example 3

Leader: I want you to look at these blocks and this peg and think about which configuration would symbolize your relationship. (*Leader has three blocks with different size holes and a peg that is obviously too big for one, nearly fits another, and fits one.*) Is your relationship the near fit, the good fit, or the impossible fit? (*All stare at the blocks.*)

Alisa: I can tell you right now. Mine is the one that does not fit at all! He wants me to fit into his little hole, and I refuse. I want to go to school, and I want to have friends that I go out with. That's why I'm in this group—to figure out what to do with my terrible fit.

Sharon: My relationship is the middle one. We nearly fit, but there are some major differences, like on religion and children. I am very religious, and he's not at all. I want three or four kids, and he's not sure if he wants any. The frustrating thing for me is that I am 36, and I don't know if I'll find someone else, so I keep trying to make this one fit; and it doesn't.

Felicia: Our fit was great at first, but now it is like the impossible fit. We fight about everything—money, sex, drugs, the house. See, I stopped doing drugs when I got pregnant, and he doesn't understand now that the baby is born why I won't go back to doing drugs. We have a terrible fit, and I don't think I can be what he wants.

Leader: That is a good point. (*Holds up peg*) This peg can be carved back enough to fit in the small hole, but there would not be much left of the peg. (*All stare at the peg.*)

Miffy: That's how I feel now. I've come a long way since my first marriage, and now I feel like if I grow any more, I won't fit in this marriage. I'm scared to grow, and I'm scared not to. I like who I am becoming.

Leader: What do you want to say to Miffy about growing?

Felicia: Keep going. We're all so proud of you! (*Miffy smiles.*)

Sharon: You don't want to stop. I admire what you have done, and I always think about you when I start to give in. I say, "Miffy did it. She had the courage to think for herself and not give in."

Leader: Let's talk about how not to frustrate yourself. All of you acknowledge the fit is not the best one, but are you productively working to resolve the problem, or are you just being upset and frustrated?

Alisa: I just frustrate myself. (*Picks up the peg and the block with the small hole; obviously frustrated as she tries to force the peg in the small hole*) I get angry at him. Why can't he change!

Miffy: I think that's what I am coming to realize. That Mickey maybe cannot change like I want him to, but I'm realizing that I am the one who is getting myself mad because I have the expectations that he be different.

Leader: What are others thinking about regarding your fit? You do not have to be frustrated and angry.

Felicia: This helps me see that I have to do something.

Leader: (*Getting a contract from the client*) Would you like to work on that now?

Felicia: Yes, I don't like living the way we do.

Leader: Felicia, I'm going to have each member ask you the same question, and I want you to answer. Miffy, ask Felicia, "What is something you can do to help you to feel better?"

Miffy: What is something you can do to help you to feel better?

Felicia: I can quit fighting with him about his drug use.

Leader: Alisa, ask her the same question.

Alisa: Felicia, what is something you can do to help you to feel better?

Felicia: (*In a very thoughtful voice*) I can get honest with myself and quit being in denial about his addiction. Uh, you know, I've never said that out loud to anyone.

Leader: Sharon, ask Felicia something about her denial or his addiction.

Sharon: Why is it hard to deal with his addiction?

Felicia: (*Crying*) My dad was an alcoholic, and I know what hell it can be. I don't want him to be an addict, but he is. Oh, what should I do? (*Sobbing*)

Leader: (*After a minute or so*) I'd say you are doing what you need to do by admitting that he is sick. Now you can get the help you need.

Miffy: (*Very kindly*) I went to AL-ANON for a year, and it helped me. I'd be glad to take you to a couple of meetings. Felicia, you can get through this, and you have taken the first step, which is to admit the truth.

Felicia: I'm so ashamed!

Leader: (*In a nurturing voice*) Wait a minute. Felicia, I want you to look at us. There is nothing to be ashamed of, and I think you can see that we all are concerned and care, but you haven't done anything to be ashamed of. (*Felicia looks and sees warm, caring faces.*)

The leader used the blocks as a way to funnel the session. By having members comment on the fit of their relationship, the session quickly funneled to **6**. By keeping the session focused on the fit, the session funneled to a greater depth, especially when the leader decided to focus on Felicia. The impact therapist had the skills, theory background, and courage to take the member deeply into her feelings. Quite often, as in this example, the Impact Therapy group leader involves the members in some way. The leader used the members to ask a repeated question which funneled the session to **4**.

Using creative or dramatic techniques when working with an individual

The Impact Therapy group leader definitely feels it is appropriate to focus on an individual and then funnel that person's work to a depth level of **6**, **4**, or even **2** or **1**. Most often when the leader does this, she uses creative and dramatic techniques that hold members' attention, or she uses members in a way that directly involves them, such as in an intensive round where a member sits in front of each member, a family sculpture, a dramatic pulling on both arms, or a role-play scene in which characters are needed.

Example 1

Leader: Do you want to work on that?

Cheryl: I want to figure what to do about my mom. Every time she calls, she's depressed, and she blames me for something. She usually starts crying and tells me what a horrible thing I did by going to my father's wedding.

Leader: (*Having used the empty chair technique before in the group*) Let's put your mom in this seat. (*Pulls up chair*) What would you say to her?

Cheryl: (*Starting to tear up*) Why can't you understand that going to my father's wedding has nothing to do with you? After all that I have done for you, why can't you say thanks, just once. That's all I ask. (*Crying*) Before you die, I would just once like you to tell me that you are proud of me.

Leader: (*Believing that Cheryl has a good Adult but is not using it in this situation with her mom*) Nina, I want you to stand in the chair and play Cheryl's mom and give Cheryl some more negative comments. Cheryl, you sit in this seat. (*Pulls up little chair*)

Nina: How can I be proud of you when you betrayed me! It's your fault I am so miserable!

Cheryl: (*Sobbing, looking up*) What do you want me to do?

Leader: Can anyone play a Nurturing Parent and talk to the Hurt Child part?

Rosemary: I think I can. (*Moving near Cheryl; in a nurturing voice*) Look you did a lot for this woman, and it was not wrong to go to that wedding. She is an unhappy person, and it is not your fault nor your responsibility to make her happy.

Cheryl: (*Looking up with a thinking look and in a slightly strong voice*) You know, you're right. You are absolutely right.

Leader: (*Motions Rosemary and Nina to go back to their seats*) Cheryl, move to this Adult chair (*pulls up another chair*) and sit in front of Daisy and say, "It's not my fault Mom is unhappy, and it is not my responsibility to make Mom happy."

Cheryl: (*In a fairly strong voice*) It's not my fault Mom is unhappy, and it is not my responsibility to make Mom happy.

Leader: Now move in front of Michelle and say the same thing. I'm going to have you say this to everyone in the group.

Cheryl: (*In a stronger voice*) It's not my fault Mom is unhappy, and it is not my responsibility to make Mom happy.

Leader: Move to Rosemary.

Cheryl: (*In a strong voice*) It's not my fault Mom is unhappy, and it is not my responsibility to make Mom happy. This is mind blowing.

Leader: In front of Karfe.

Cheryl: (*In a very strong voice*) It's not my fault. She's got to make herself happy. I can't do it. You know what I am realizing. My problem is not with my mom but with my little girl who has always wanted her attention.

Leader: (*Noticing that Alexia is tearing*) Alexia, are you okay?

Alexia: This is so similar to me and my mom.

Leader: We'll spend a couple of more minutes with Cheryl, and then we'll come to you. Are any others of you relating to this?

Nina: I am. I see that I've still got work to do on my mother. I thought I was done, but I can feel I'm not. If we have time, I'd like to talk about it.

In this example, the leader funneled the session to **4** or **3** by using the members to play different parts. Even though the focus was on Cheryl, it was intense enough and dramatic enough so as to engage everyone. The use of the chairs was helpful to get Cheryl to see what she was doing. Other members, such as Alexia and Nina, could put themselves in Cheryl's place. Cheryl got to hear herself in her Adult when she did the round where she sat in front of each person. The impact therapist made a lot happen in a short period of time and saw that at least two more members wanted to work. (It has been my experience when I have funneled a session to **5** or below that other members get in touch with their issues, and then they want to work.)

In the next example, the leader used the idea of tapes that need changing or editing to focus and funnel the session. From the comments of the members, the impact therapist felt that focusing on individuals could be productive and efficient since each person had something to work on. The leader went right to the work rather than discussing the issues for a while.

Example 2

Leader: I want each of you to realize something. When you were growing up, you made a tape about yourself, and now you play that tape in your head. (*Holds up a cassette tape to her ear as if she is listening to it*) I want you to think about what is on your tape. I think most of you have lots of negative things on your tape due to your home life and other experiences that you had early in life. One purpose of this group is to help you to edit your old tapes and make new tapes. (*Puts brand new tapes with members' names on them in the center of the room*) Each of you can get a tape and start making a new one, or you can continue to play the old ones—it's your choice. (*Members stare at the tapes.*) I'd like you first to think about what is on your tape, and then we'll talk about making your new tape.

Rex: I have a huge segment that says, "I'll never amount to anything. I'm always going to be a screw up."

Rod: I'm unattractive and unappealing. No matter how many compliments I get or how much I workout, I still feel that I am fat and dumpy like I was in middle school. I win body building contests and everything, but I still carry that old image.

Gina: Feeling unattractive is also one of mine. My biggest one is that I'm dumb and stupid. I still get nervous when I go to meetings with my husband who is a lawyer because I worry that I'll say something stupid. I always feel that everyone is smarter than me.

Betty:	I'll tell you one that I have that is interfering right now in my life, and that is "I can't write!" I'm trying to do a dissertation, and I can't get myself to do it. There's lots of fear.
Bree:	I have all kinds of tapes about what a woman should be, which is wife and mother; and I am neither of those. I often feel bad for the way I'm living, yet I like being single. I may get married, but it is not a big need of mine. I think I am clear on this, but then there will be something on television or a comment from Mom or Dad, and I'm wiped out.
Leader:	Each of you look at your new tape. You can make new tapes based upon your views now rather than what you were taught or experienced as a kid. Who wants to work on editing and remaking his or her tape?
Betty:	(*Goes and gets her tape and then sits back down*) I do because I want to get this damn dissertation finished.
Leader:	Tell us more about you and writing.
Betty:	I have this fear that it'll be wrong, and my committee will yell at me and ridicule me.
Leader:	Do you have a bunch of bad committee members?
Betty:	No, not really. My chairperson is Dana, and she's very supportive and encouraging; and the others are decent. I don't know what this is about. I know that I am a perfectionist. I always have been. I feel that everything should be perfect, and the first time my major professor turned back my paper with all these red marks, I felt devastated. I felt like I was a freshman again.
Leader:	What do you mean? (*Looks around at others who seem interested and puzzled. The leader is thinking of ways to involve them but feels that Betty still needs to funnel to a deeper level.*)
Betty:	(*Wipes away some tears*) When I went off to school, my dad made me write home every week. He always wrote back and sent my letter back with red corrections marked all over it regarding grammar, spelling, paragraph construction, and all kinds of other things.
Leader:	Wait a minute. Do you think that is normal?
Betty:	He said he was just trying to help me become educated. It didn't feel good, but I probably did learn to write better. I actually moved back home the second year because I

didn't want to write those letters. I was even afraid when I went off to graduate school he would make me write, but he never said anything. He tells me to send him drafts, and he'll help me.

Leader: (*To the group, knowing that their comments will be thought provoking and supportive*) What is your reaction to this?

Gina: I am flabbergasted! I have never heard of such cruel treatment. It's no wonder you are afraid of writing. I'd be too if my dad had done that to me!

Rex: It helps me to see that we can't see what is normal for ourselves. Betty, there's nothing normal about that, but I could tell you thought it was sort of normal. I started thinking where my ideas about being a screw-up came from, and my dad and grandmother played a big part in helping me make my tapes. (*Betty is listening very intently to all the comments.*)

Bree: It's no wonder we believe what we do. Someone pounded stuff in our heads. My stuff is different than yours, and I can see how you have come to believe you can't write. My problem is I can't see mine so clearly. (*Turns to leader*) What will help Betty or me get over our beliefs? I want to change my tapes; I have to! (*Walks to the center and gets her tape*)

Leader: (*Pulls up three chairs, one being a child's chair; puts a book in one chair*) Betty, when you go to sit in front of your computer (*points at the book indicating that it represents a computer*), you take the little girl who was and is afraid of Dad (*pulls little chair in front of the chair with a book*) and try to write, and very little comes out. Your Adult is back here somewhere with lots of knowledge and desire to get on with your life, but the little girl goes to the computer. (*Betty is staring at the chairs. Members are looking at Betty and the chairs. Some are obviously into their own issues.*)

Betty: I don't know why, but I am feeling lighter or something. What would happen if I sat in the Adult chair?

Leader: We'll do both. Sit, first, in the Child chair, and then sit in the Adult chair. Tune into your thoughts and feelings as you sit in both seats.

Betty: (*Sits in both chairs, taking some time in each seat, and then goes back to her seat*) The Child felt very familiar. I felt fear and had all kinds of thoughts about not being able to do it. I also had images of my father. In the Adult seat, I almost felt blank.

Leader: (*To Betty and everyone*) That's what making new tapes is about. You have to have an Adult perspective on things or else your old tape will play.

Betty: That's exactly right!! I am a decent writer, partly due probably to my dad. I just need to get him out of the loop.

Leader: Good point. Let's do this. I want you to sit in the Child chair and get ready to scoot it up to the computer. As you do, Rod, I want you, representing her dad, to stand between Betty in her Child chair and the computer. (*They do this.*)

Betty: This is exactly what I do, and then fear comes over me! What should I do?

Leader: I'm going to have each member ask you, while sitting in the Adult seat, that question. (*Betty moves to the Adult chair.*)

Bree: What do you need to do when you go to write your dissertation?

Betty: Get my dad out of there. Realize that I am not writing this for my dad. Believe me, the members of my committee are much easier than my dad. (*Leader points to Gina.*)

Gina: What do you believe on your new tape about you and writing your dissertation?

Betty: I can write. I have had articles published. It does not have to be perfect. Boy, is that a big one.

Leader: Look at each person and say that sentence.

Betty: (*Looking at Gina*) It does not have to be perfect.

Betty: (*Looking at Rex*) It does not have to be perfect.

Betty: (*Looking at Rod*) It does not have to be perfect! It is not even expected to be.

Betty: (*Looking at Bree*) It does not have to be perfect! Write something and then make the corrections as they are suggested.

Leader: Let's go back to the round about finishing your dissertation. Look at Rex.

Rex: What do you need to do to finish your dissertation?

Betty: I need to keep an Adult perspective and see it as something that I want to do and can do. There does not have to be any fear. (*Smiling*) All my fear comes from my Child, and she doesn't have any business trying to write a dissertation. (*All laugh.*)

Leader: Do we need to do some more, or do you feel you have enough for now?

Betty: This has helped a great deal. I'll let you know next week if the Adult made it to the computer.

Leader: Let me do a quick round of what you are thinking as a result of Betty's work, and then we'll see who wants to work next.

Gina: This was real helpful for me. That little chair will stand out for me. That's who I take to my husband's functions. My tape comes from not graduating from college; and when I stopped and thought about it, the reason I didn't was because I went home to take care of my mom. Then I got married and worked to put my husband through law school. I absolutely need to update my tape. (*Goes and gets her new tape*)

Rex: The power of the Child! That's what hit me. My Child is big and does me no good at all. I don't know how to get rid of it though.

Rod:	I want help in seeing me for who I am and not who I was. Betty's work makes me more determined to get into the present. It was obvious from watching that the past can cripple you. It does me.
Bree:	I just want to figure out what I do believe about being a woman. I'm ready to work on that if we're ready.
Leader:	Sure. (*Puts old tape in little chair*) Tell us what all is on that tape about what a woman is.
Bree:	I was taught that a woman....

The impact therapist used the idea of tapes to get members to tune into messages they play inside their heads. Members quickly got into some of their issues, and the leader decided to funnel an individual's work. As Betty was initially exploring her issue about writing, the members mostly watched. As she funneled, the leader got the members involved in a number of ways; also, Betty's work was at a deep enough level (*4* or *3*) to cause members to reflect on their on issues as well as follow Betty's work. The members were asked to share their reactions to Betty's story about her dad; and then the leader, wanting to have impact on Betty and the others, used the chairs and the make believe computer to dramatize Betty's situation. Many of the members projected themselves into the chairs even though their issues were different from Betty's. The leader, thinking of visual images and ways of using the members, had Betty try to move to the computer but experience her dad being in the way. This more than likely caused members to think about what is in their way. By using the repeating round, Betty was able to hear herself come from the Adult and, thus, strengthen that ego state.

When Betty was finished, the leader first heard from everyone before starting to work on Bree. He did this because he wanted to give everyone a chance to comment, and he was interested in hearing what had been stirred up in each of the members.

In this entire section on funneling, I showed a variety of techniques that impact therapists use to funnel the session. First and foremost, the leader sees herself as responsible for making sure the session does funnel. She knows that, in order to do this, she will have to keep the members focused and not let them go from topic to topic or person to person without going deeper. The leader uses cut-off skills, theories, exercises, props, chairs, rounds, movement, and creative and dramatic scenes to funnel sessions to meaningful levels. There are times when the leader funnels a topic and has members sharing at a productive level, and there are times when the leader funnels the work of a member to a much deeper level by focusing the group for an extended period on that member only.

SUMMARY

Purpose, plan, focus, and funnel (**PPFF**) are the essential steps that an impact therapist follows when leading a group. The leader has to be clear as to the purpose of the group and then plans for the entire group and each session. Good planning usually insures that the group will be beneficial. The key to a good group is in focusing because, without focusing, the group usually drifts along. The impact therapist believes that it is his responsibility to focus and funnel the group. Impact in groups most often comes as a result of the session funneling below **7**. The leader uses many different techniques to funnel the session on either a topic or an individual.

References

Carkuff, R. R. (1987). *The art of helping* (6th ed.). Amherst, MA: Human Resource Development Press.

Carroll, M. R. (1986). *Group work: Leading in the here and now* [Film]. Alexandria, VA: American Counseling Association.

Cormier, W. H., & Cormier, L. S. (1991). *Interviewing strategies for helpers: Fundamental skills and cognitive behavioral interventions* (3rd ed.). Pacific Grove, CA: Brooks/Cole.

Cormier, L. S., & Hackney, H. (1993). *The professional counselor* (2nd ed.). Boston: Allyn and Bacon.

Corey, G. (1990). *The theory and practice of group counseling* (3rd ed.). Pacific Grove, CA: Brooks/Cole.

Egan, G. (1994). *The skilled helper* (5th ed.). Pacific Grove, CA: Brooks/Cole.

Ellis, A. (1962). *Reason and emotion in psychotherapy*. New York: Lyle Stuart.

Gladding, S. T. (1988). *Counseling: A comprehensive profession*. Columbus, OH: Merrill.

Ivey, A. E. (1994). *Intentional interviewing and counseling* (3rd ed.). Pacific Grove: Brooks/Cole.

Jacobs, E. E. (1992). *Creative counseling techniques: An illustrated guide*. Odessa, FL: Psychological Assessment Resources.

Jacobs, E. E., Harvill, R. L., & Masson, R. L. (1994). *Group counseling: Strategies and skills* (2nd ed.). Pacific Grove, CA: Brooks/Cole.

Jewett, C. (1994). *Helping children cope with separation and loss* (2nd ed.). Harvard, MA: Harvard Common Press.

Okun, B. F. (1992). *Effective helping: Interviewing and counseling techniques* (4th ed.). Pacific Grove, CA: Brooks/Cole.

Passons, W. R. (1975). *Gestalt approaches in counseling*. New York: Holt, Rinehart, & Winston.

Rando, T. (1984). *Grief, dying, and death*. Champaign, IL: Research Press.

Rogers, C. (1961). *Client centered therapy*. Boston: Houghton Mifflin.

Stewart, I., & Joines, V. (1987). *TA today*. Chapel Hill, NC: Lifespace Publishing.

Walen, S., DiGiuseppe, R., & Wessler, R. (1992). *A practitioner's guide to Rational-Emotive Therapy* (2nd ed.). New York: Oxford University Press.

Worden, J. W. (1991). *Grief counseling and grief therapy: A handbook for the mental health practitioner* (2nd ed.). New York: Springer.

Yalom, I. (1985). *The theory and practice of group psychotherapy* (3rd ed.). New York: Basic Books.